EXILE IN ISRAEL

A Personal Journey with the Palestinians

Dr Runa Mackay

First published 1995

ISBN 0 947988 75 0

Copyright © 1995 Dr Runa Mackay

Wild Goose Publications, Unit 15, Six Harmony Row, Glasgow G513BA

Wild Goose Publications is the publishing division of the Iona Community.
Scottish Charity No. SC003794. Limited Company Reg. No. SCO96243.

Distributed in Australia and New Zealand by Willow Connection Pty Ltd,
Unit 7A, 3-9 Kenneth Road, Manly Vale NSW 2093.
Permission to reproduce any part of this work in Australia or New Zealand
should be sought from Willow Connection.

A catalogue record for this book is available from the British Library.

Cover design by Iona L Macgregor. The front cover image is based on an
interpretation of the Palestinian flag.

Printed by The Cromwell Press Ltd, Melksham, Wilts.

For my three sisters whose constant love and
support sustained me and enabled me,
and for Samiha whose friendship lightened
all my days in Lebanon.

I would like to thank my niece Anna Woolverton
for her computer expertise
and Moira Baikie for drawing the map.

CONTENTS

FOREWORD

Take us "outside the camp", Lord.
Outside holiness.
Out to where soldiers gamble,
and thieves curse, and nations clash
at the cross-roads of the world.

Rev. George F MacLeod, *The Whole Earth Shall Cry Glory*
(Wild Goose Publications, p. 45), © 1985 The Iona Community.

INTRODUCTION

Why would a Christian medical missionary doctor from Edinburgh devote her life to working for the Palestinians? When we read Dr Runa Mackay's moving answer, you will see why this book is indeed a treasure to read, its pages embodying a half-century of devotion to the people of the Holy Land.

I have always been in awe of Runa's commitment. I am now even more impressed by her clarity of thought. Her book has deepened my limited understanding, helping me see the wider picture of the triangle linking all Palestinians together. Having lived in Galilee, in Lebanon and in the Occupied Territories, she bears witness for Palestinians living within that trinity — in Israel's 'Green Line', in the diaspora of exile and under occupation. She shows how all three, separated by geography, are united by a common history, struggle and future. The resilience, courage, generosity and warmth of a nation living under extremes of wretchedness and confronting the greatest of odds comes through in page after page of this remarkable book.

Compared to what Runa has lived through, mine has been a pale shadow. In 1982, I worked among the Palestinians of Beirut's Sabra-Shatila camps, like her, because I was a Christian and because I was a doctor. Many of those camp-dwellers were exiles forced to flee Galilee, the region within today's Israel in which Runa first worked. Within the camp, we had no contact with those who remained in Galilee, no direct means of knowing what became of Galilee and what Galilee's Palestinians felt towards the diaspora. Runa has helped fill that gap. When news of the Sabra-Shatila massacre reached Galilee and the world later that year, she tells us Galilee grieved and mourned the murder of friends and relatives. In much the same way, I witnessed how Lebanon's Palestinians rejoiced when they first heard of the Intifada uprising in late 1987 in Gaza and the rest of the Occupied Territories. And I can verify how Gaza reacted to the continued plight of those in exile in the Lebanon.

Runa remains with the Palestinians even when she returns to Britain. A few years after some of us founded the charity, Medical Aid for Palestinians (MAP), in the wake of the Sabra-Shatila massacres, I recall being speechless when I first heard a new member speak these words at a MAP public meeting: 'I have joined MAP after having retired from thirty years of work as a full-time medical missionary in Palestine.' Runa has since been a pillar of strength and an inspiration to all of us. Tireless as ever, calm and steady in a crisis, she now chairs MAP's branch in Scotland and joins us on the board of management. We know God has provided a true friend for the Palestinian people.

This book is a celebration of faith, hope and love for, and of, a dispossessed people. Through Runa, we are all challenged to meet God's call to serve our brothers and sisters in a still troubled part of the world. For Runa's friends, genuine peace and justice can only come to the Middle East when all of them can come home to end their exile and to secure their right to statehood, freed from occupation and domination.

Dr Swee Chai ANG (FRCS)
Consultant Orthopaedic Surgeon
1995

(author of *From Beirut to Jerusalem*, published by Grafton Books, UK, 1989)

1

THE BEGINNING

'Take time to be, to feel,
to listen to the stories, dreams and thoughts
of those who have no voice.
They're wounded for the want of being listened to:
they cry
and too few hear;
they slowly die
and too few mourn.'

Kate Compston, 'Seeds of Hope' [1]

'Then they called me a refugee' — these were Abu Hassan's bitter words which have been engraved on my heart since 1987 when I heard them in Qasmiyeh, a Palestinian refugee 'camp' in south Lebanon. Abu Hassan was a Beduin and he used to ride freely over the hills of Galilee — until the day in 1948, when he and all his tribe had to flee north into Lebanon to escape the advancing Israeli army. In order to explain how I came to be living with Palestinian refugees in a camp in south Lebanon in 1987, I have to go back some seventy years.

My early years were spent in Hull where my father practised as an eye surgeon. At the beginning of the Second World War I went up to Edinburgh to study medicine — following in my father's footsteps — and I graduated in 1944. When my father had been a medical student, he had worked in the Livingstone Dispensary in Edinburgh's Cowgate, the poorest area of Edinburgh at that time, and, naturally, when I became a student I too went to work there. The Livingstone Dispensary was run by the Edinburgh Medical Missionary Society (EMMS), which had been founded in 1841 to train doctors to serve overseas as medical missionaries. At first the assistance offered to students was mainly financial but in 1895 a medical mission dispensary was opened in the Grassmarket area by one of the directors of the society. As the years passed the dispensary was adopted by EMMS and was used by the university for the training of its medical students, both those who were planning to be medical missionaries and others, like me, who had no thought of ever working overseas. In my student days, in the 1940s, there was a busy outpatient clinic with a pharmacy and a dental surgery. Short daily services were held, as well as a Sunday School, women's meetings and Bible classes, all of which activities the students shared. It was a valuable experience for me. I would plod up and down the tenement stairs visiting patients and I still remember one little boy who was very ill with pneumonia. In those days there were no antibiotics, not even penicillin. I told the medical superintendent of the dispensary, Dr Lechler, how worried and helpless I felt about the child. He said to me, 'You can only do your best, the rest is in God's hands', advice which has stood me in good stead throughout my medical career.

The work of the Livingstone Dispensary was eventually made redundant, with the coming of the National Health Service, and closed down. The work of EMMS in helping to finance prospective medical missionaries, however, continued until government grants made such financial help unnecessary. The student hostel remained open until 1989. EMMS also had the responsibility of running two hospitals, one in Nazareth and one in Damascus.

Medical work began in Nazareth in 1861 by Dr Kaloost Vartan. At that time Nazareth was a small town in Palestine in the Vilayat of Beirut in the Ottoman Empire. Dr Vartan was born in Istanbul, capital of the Ottoman Empire, in 1835 to Armenian Episcopalian parents. He could speak Armenian, Turkish and English and was employed as a translator by a British officer in the Russian/Ottoman War of 1853. His work took him among the sick and wounded so he vowed to become a doctor. At the end of the war he was able to study in Edinburgh with the help of EMMS. In 1860, in the wake of the terrible massacres of Christians by Druze in Mount Lebanon, Dr Vartan was sent by The London Society for Sending Aid to the Protestants of Syria, to help the survivors who had fled to Beirut. Later he was invited to go to Nazareth and to open a dispensary there. In 1865 he was adopted as the 'agent' of EMMS in Nazareth. He soon saw the need for a hospital and presented plans to the Society and, in 1871, the first EMMS Hospital in Nazareth was opened, with eighteen beds. The site of the present hospital was purchased from the Turkish government in 1906. There were financial problems at first and then when the hospital was nearly completed the First World War broke out. The building was commandeered by the Turkish army and vandalised. By 1924 it had been repaired and was reopened and continues to this day to serve the people of Nazareth and Galilee. The hospital in Damascus was opened in 1884 but was forced to close down in 1957 after the Suez War.

The work of EMMS was thus known to me, but, when I qualified in 1944, I was set on making my career in paediatrics. The state of Israel had been declared in 1948, but that fact and the resultant flight and plight of the Palestinians meant little to me. The horrors of the Holocaust and the death of six million Jews were much more vivid.

I had worked as professorial medical registrar in the Children's Hospital in Manchester since 1952. By 1954 I knew that this work was coming to an end and I had to decide what my next step should be. Unexpectedly a letter came from Dr John Tester in the EMMS Hospital in Nazareth — since 1948 in the state of Israel — asking if I knew of anyone who could do a locum for him while he went on six-months leave. I was free so I rather tentatively offered to go, pointing out that I was a paediatrician and, although I was a Christian, I had never thought of myself as a missionary — my offer was immediately accepted and in March 1955 I flew out to Israel, to start work at the Nazareth Hospital, originally for six months, but I eventually stayed for thirty years. My six-month contract was extended to one year and then Dr Doris Wilson, who had looked after the women and children for many years, decided to move out to work in a village under the auspices of the Arab Episcopal Church. She asked me if I would consider succeeding her. I had enjoyed all the jobs I had done but had not considered any of them long term, but now I knew that work in Nazareth could become my life's work, God willing, and so it proved to be.

The medical work was heavy and kept me very busy — at times in the early days there would only be two of us looking after more than a hundred inpatients and many more outpatients in the hospital. However, as ninety-nine per cent of the patients and the local staff were Palestinian Arabs, one absorbed the history, the culture and the ethos of Palestine, day-by-day. We were often invited to weddings in Nazareth and the villages of Galilee and everybody visited everybody else at all the religious feasts, whether Christian or Muslim. My life thus became intricately bound up with that of the Palestinians.

1   *Circles of Silence* (Darton, Longman & Todd, London, 1994, p. 43)

2

HISTORY OF PALESTINE

*'The Lord says, "The land is Mine and you are
but aliens and My tenants."'*

Leviticus 25.23 (New International Version of the Holy Bible)[1]

The Palestinians are a people descended from the earliest re-
corded inhabitants of the area, who intermarried with the
Philistines, Jews and Arabs who came from the Arabian penin-
sula. In the days of the Roman Empire, Palestine was the land to
the west of the Jordan River and the east bank was called Urdun.
In the time of Christ the Jews had been in the majority but, after
the Jewish revolt against the Romans in AD 132, the majority were
slaughtered and the rest scattered. With the fall of the Roman
Empire in the middle of the fifth century Palestine became part of
the Eastern Byzantine Empire, a Greek kingdom with a Roman
law code and a Christian faith, until the coming of Islam in the
seventh century. The Muslim armies captured Jerusalem in AD 638,
the people of Syria and Palestine began to speak Arabic and ninety
per cent converted to Islam. The ten per cent who chose to remain Christian and the Jews who still lived there were treated
well as 'People of the Book' — they only had to pay a 'head tax'.
In 1099 the Crusaders recaptured Jerusalem from the Muslims —
and massacred the entire population of the city, Jewish and Muslim. They established a kingdom in Palestine based in Jerusalem
but in 1187 they were defeated and expelled from Jerusalem by
Saladin. They were eventually expelled from Palestine in 1291
when their last stronghold, the port of Acre, was recaptured by
the Muslims. In 1516 the Ottomans took Palestine and Syria from
the Mamelukes of Egypt, put Jerusalem under direct rule from
Constantinople, made the south of Palestine part of the Sanjuk of
Jerusalem and the west of Palestine part of the Vilayat of Beirut.
The Ottoman Empire lasted for 400 years until it was overthrown
in the First World War.

General Allenby entered Jerusalem in 1917 and then, at the
Treaty of Versailles, Britain was given the League of Nations Man-

date for Palestine. By the terms of the Mandate, Britain promised to administer the country according to the principle that the wellbeing and development of the inhabitants form a sacred trust of civilisation. However also enshrined in the articles of the Mandate were the Mandatory's responsibility to ensure the establishment of the 'Jewish National Home' and to facilitate Jewish immigration.

Theodore Herzl, the founder of the modern Zionist movement in 1896, had not, at first, been particular about where a Jewish state should be located but, in the end, he chose Palestine because of its emotional appeal to the Jewish masses of Eastern Europe, although it was opposed by the rabbis. In the First World War the Allies needed the support of the Zionists against Germany, so in 1917 the British Foreign Secretary, Lord Balfour, wrote to Lord Rothschild his famous letter which became known as the Balfour Declaration: 'His Majesty's Government view with favour the establishment in Palestine of a National Home for the Jewish people, and will use their best endeavours to facilitate the achievement of this object, it being clearly understood that nothing shall be done which may prejudice the civil and religious rights of the existing non-Jewish communities in Palestine, or the rights and political status enjoyed by Jews in any other country.' But Balfour admitted that, 'in Palestine we do not propose even to go through the form of consulting the wishes of the present inhabitants of the country. The four Great Powers are committed to Zionism, and Zionism, be it right or wrong, good or bad, is rooted in age-long traditions, in future hopes of far profounder import than the desires and prejudices of the 700,000 Arabs who now inhabit that ancient land.'[2]

So began the stormy years of British mandatory rule in Palestine. Jewish immigration continued slowly but remorselessly and although, at first, the Palestinians were not unduly worried they gradually came to realise what was happening — that their country was being taken over by the Jews with British connivance. Large tracts of land in Palestine — owned by absentee landlords in Lebanon — were sold, over the heads of the Palestinian peasants, to the Jewish Agency.

There were revolts and massacres, government commissions and White Papers but the outbreak of the Second World War and then the horrors of the Holocaust changed 'the goal posts'. Many

Jews from Eastern Europe had fought with the Allies, six million had died in the Holocaust and the survivors had nowhere to go. Europe, including Britain, was impoverished and relying on US aid and the US had closed its doors, admitting only 4,787 survivors in 1946. It seemed that the only place they could go to was Palestine. Britain was helpless to resolve the conflicting claims and in 1947 decided to turn over the whole question of the future of Palestine to the United Nations. After extensive hearings the UN recommended the partition of Palestine into an Arab state and a Jewish state, with the internationalisation of Jerusalem. The Jewish state would include the coastal plain (except for Arab Jaffa), part of Galilee and most of the Negev.

The Jews accepted the plan, because, as Ben Gurion, Israel's first Prime Minister, had said in 1938, 'When we become a strong power after the establishment of the state we will abolish partition and spread throughout the whole of Palestine.'[3] The Arabs rejected the plan, much to the relief of the Jews. Menachim Begin said, 'My greatest worry was that the Arabs might accept the UN plan then we would have been left with a Jewish state so small that it could not absorb all the Jews of the world.'[4] The Jews could now set in motion, on the pretext that the Arabs had rejected a UN decision, their carefully laid plans to dislodge the Palestinians by fair means or foul and extend the proposed UN boundaries by military force and thus create a Jewish state.

Fighting started as soon as the details of the Partition Plan were announced. The Jews had a well-organised and well-armed force — the Haganah, plus two terrorist organisations, the Irgun, formed in 1938 and headed by Menachem Begin and the Stern Gang led by Yitzhak Shamir. Their combined membership numbered 30,000, plus 30,000 reservists. A large supply of armaments came in regularly, though clandestinely, from Czechoslovakia. The Jews also had the great advantage of unity of command and interior battle lines so they could switch men around as needed. The disorganised Palestinians could only muster 2,500 men, however they created the Arab Liberation Army consisting of 4,996 volunteers from various countries under the command of the Arab League Military Committee in Damascus. Nevertheless they were poorly armed, Czechoslovakia having reneged on an agreement to supply them with arms. The Arab League states said they would help the Palestinians but they had no intention of sending in their own regular armies and, anyway, between them they had less than 14,000 men. By April 1948 the vital port city of Haifa fell to the Jews setting off a chain reaction of alarm throughout Palestine.

Cedar was nine years old in 1948 and living in Haifa. She recalls how she and her eight-year-old brother were put on a vegetable lorry travelling to Nazareth and told to lie flat until they reached the house of their grandparents in Nazareth. They were absolutely terrified, hearing shooting all around them and not understanding what was happening to them. They arrived safely and, some time later, their father joined them having escaped from Haifa in a British Navy ship which was helping to evacuate Palestinians from Haifa and taking them to Beirut. Cedar's father managed to jump ship in Acre and so reached Nazareth.

By 13 May Jaffa was also captured and the next day, all British troops having been evacuated, the British Mandate came to an end, and the leaders of the Jewish community proclaimed the birth of the state of Israel. Immediately the Arab states sent in their undersized regular armies. The success of the Zionists and the expulsion of the Palestinians had really alarmed the Arab world and made them fearful that they would be the next for invasion.
 The fighting dragged on, but, by the end of the year, Israel had signed armistice agreements with Egypt, Syria, Lebanon and Transjordan. Israel now had control of all the parts of Palestine which had been allotted in the Partition Plan, plus a corridor from Tel Aviv to the western half of Jerusalem.
 Soon afterwards King Abdulla of Jordan annexed the rest of Palestine to Transjordan creating thereby the kingdom of Jordan and Palestine was no more. The human cost of the war had left several hundred Palestinians dead, 726,000 had fled and 160,000 were incorporated into the new state of Israel. Thus began the saga which the Palestinians call 'the Catastrophe', their exile and what the world would refer to as the 'problem' of these refugees.

1 (Copyright © 1973, 1978, 1984 by International Bible Society. Used by permission of Hodder & Stoughton Ltd. All rights reserved.)
2 Peter Mansfield, *The Arabs* (Penguin, London, 1985, p. 189)
3 Michael Palumbo, *The Palestinian Catastrophe* (Faber & Faber, London, 1987, p. 32)
4 Palumbo, *The Palestinian Catastrophe*, p.34

3

REFUGEES

'You, who are Gentiles by birth ... excluded from citizenship in Israel, without hope and without God in the world ... now have been brought near through the blood of Christ. For He Himself is our peace, who has made the two one and has destroyed the barrier, the dividing wall of hostility.'

Ephesians 2.11-15 (New International Version of the Holy Bible)[1]

In wars people have often been forced to flee to escape the fighting, taking refuge elsewhere, until, with the cessation of hostilities, they could return to their homes. The exodus of the Palestinians in the war of 1947-49 was of quite a different kind. It involved the systematic expulsion of most of the Palestinian population into exile and then the refusal to let them return.

It used to be claimed that the Palestinians fled because their leaders told them to. Recent release of classified archives of the period have shown that quite the opposite was the case. The Arab leaders tried to encourage the people to stay, while the Zionists encouraged them to go, by a systematic policy of intimidation and killing. Michael Palumbo writes, 'No amount of pseudo-academic argument about an "irrational panic syndrome" or "the loss of community infrastructure" can obscure the fact that most of the Palestinians did not leave their towns or villages until they were invaded by an Israeli army that subjected them to a reign of terror.'[2]

It has been revealed that the self-confessed ideology of the Zionists was to get rid of the Arab population and not to allow them to return. This they did by an organized campaign of terror; the spreading of rumours and psychological warfare by radio and loud-speaker and lethal attacks on civilians in the villages. They carried out sieges of the larger towns and then expelled the people at gunpoint even though they had surrendered.

In November 1947 with the announcement of the UN Partition Plan and the approaching end of the British Mandate, people with the means to do so started to leave for Beirut and elsewhere never imagining that it would be for good. This early exodus of the more educated and better off Palestinians left the poorer people like the villagers, the townspeople and the port workers in Haifa feeling very apprehensive and vulnerable.

The Arab leadership did not advise them nor tell them what to do as they themselves were divided. Haj Ameen Husseini, the *Mufti* (the head of the Supreme Muslim Council) of Jerusalem and Head of the Arab Higher Committee was in a state of open hostility with the commander-in-chief of the Arab Liberation Army, Fowzi al Qawqaji.

The news of the massacre of 250 defenceless villagers, including women and children, at Deir Yassin, near Jerusalem, by the Irgun and Stern Jewish terrorist gangs in April 1948 was a very powerful incentive to people to flee.

Hatim was eleven years old and he remembers the discussion in the family — should they go or should they stay. His family and the elders of the village, Araby Batoff, decided to go, and the only thing he was determined to take with him was his pet bird in its cage, so they set off, only to be told that the border into Lebanon was closed and they must return to the village where they surrendered to the Israeli army. Thirty young men from the village were promptly taken away and not heard of for six months. All the livestock, the cows, goats and chickens were rounded up and put in a pound, for the use of the soldiers, and the villagers had to manage as best they could. They became 'Israeli Arabs', and live there to this day. I have talked to many of the refugees who did flee to Lebanon and each one, referring to his family and immediate neighbours said, 'We decided to go.'

Mufid, who lived in a small town, told me that there was so much fighting nearby, his father had eventually said 'We will have to go', and in the end the whole town left and is now off the map. Never did any of them say that they were ordered to go by the Arab leadership.

Father Elias Chacour writes most poignantly in his book *Blood Brothers* about his village of Biram in the north of Galilee. In 1948 the entire population of the village was driven out and subsequently a kibbutz was built on their land. In 1950, living as 'internal refugees' in a nearby village, they petitioned the Supreme Court of Israel for the right to return to their homes. Their petition was granted but, when they joyously hurried back, they were driven away by soldiers standing guard. They realised that this new state of Israel was a nation where the military ruled, ignoring the will of the country's judges and law makers. In 1951 they tried again and once more the court granted them permission to return — the elders presented the court order to the soldiers. This time the commanding officer did not argue, he just said, 'We need time to pull out, come back on the 25th,' — Christmas Day. The whole village marched back to receive their long awaited Christmas present — as they stood on the hill overlooking the village they witnessed the army destroying their homes with tanks, shells and bulldozers until there was nothing left but the ruins of the church. For so called security reasons the military had defied the Supreme Court.[3]

I was in the south of Lebanon in July 1993 when the Israeli airforce bombed the Lebanese villages around the Palestinian camp where I was living. The aim was to frighten the villagers to petition their government to stop Hizbullah — the 'Party of God', backed by Iran — attacking Israel. The result was a massive precipitate flight of Lebanese and Palestinian civilians to the north, leaving everything behind them, although they knew only too well what had happened to the Palestinians in 1948. They thought that Israel had expansionist ideas so might annex the whole of south Lebanon. Those fleeing had nowhere to go and many slept in their cars or in the streets of Beirut. Fortunately the campaign was quickly brought to an end and the people were able to return home.

Why did many refugees never return home? It has often been said that the Arab governments kept the Palestinians as refugees to use them as pawns in a political game. It is true that the Arab host governments did not want the refugees to stay, only Jordan gave them citizenship across the board while Lebanon only gave this status to Christians. Only when Israel refused them repatriation did they become pawns — hostages to the future when Palestine could once again be on the map.

The Israelis had never had any intention of allowing the Palestinians to return — Ben Gurion said categorically on 16 June 1948, 'They shall not return, this is our policy, they shall not return.'[4]

The Zionist plan to bring thousands of Jewish immigrants to Israel would have been almost impossible without the houses, the land and the businesses of the Palestinians who had owned fifty per cent of the citrus orchards, ninety per cent of the olive groves and 10,000 shops, stores and other businesses.

The Arab host government wanted to be relieved of the burden of caring for their unwanted guests and pressed for their return even though it would be to Israeli-occupied territory. However the Israelis had no intention of allowing repatriation. For half-a-century the Zionists had been awaiting this opportunity to get rid of the Arabs and, having done so, no argument from friend or neutral observer would persuade them otherwise. The UN mediator, Count Bernadotte, worked tirelessly, hoping that their return might be part of a comprehensive peace plan but he paid with his life on 17 September 1948, assassinated by the Stern Gang near Jerusalem. His peace plan died with him.

As the years passed the Israelis claimed that they favoured resettlement for the refugees in neighbouring countries. However this must be questioned. As long as the refugees remained an unresolved 'problem', there would be tensions in the area which could be used to ignite new wars of conquest to Israel's benefit. So the refugees remained in the camps in Gaza, Jordan, Lebanon and Syria and, as had been forecast, over the years they became radicalized.

1   (Copyright ©1973, 1978, 1984 by International Bible Society. Used by permission of Hodder & Stoughton Ltd. All rights reserved.)
2   Michael Palumbo, *The Palestinian Catastrophe* (Faber & Faber, London, 1987, introduction, p. 18)
3   Elias Chacour, *Blood Brothers* (Kingsway Publications, Eastbourne, 1984, p. 71, 80-83)
4   Palumbo, *The Palestinian Catastrophe*, p. 145

4

NAZARETH

'I thank Jesus Christ, our Lord, who has given me strength that He considered me faithful, appointing me to His service.'

1 Timothy 1.12 (New International Version of the Holy Bible)[1]

My involvement with the Middle East began in 1955 with my arrival in Nazareth, when the state of Israel was only seven years old. By then the city of Nazareth, which has been a Christian town since the time of Christ, had a population of 40,000, seventy per cent Christian and thirty per cent Muslim. We also served the villages of Galilee which were Christian, Muslim, Druze or of mixed religions. In 1948 the total Arab population of the new state of Israel had been about 160,000, mostly based in Galilee, but with a few in the 'Little Triangle' (near the Jordanian border), Lydda and Ramleh.

In those early years in Nazareth I heard many stories of what had happened in 1948. Nazareth itself had been spared by order of the Prime Minister, David Ben Gurion. When the people of Nazareth heard that towns nearby were falling into the hands of the Israelis they too were ready to flee but were stopped and forced to return to the city. The Israeli commander recalled, 'We had specific instructions from Ben Gurion not to harm anything and to avoid any possibility of looting or desecration of churches or monasteries.'[2] The mayor and the Christian clerics surrendered, with the request that the civilian population should not be forced to flee and their request was granted. The Israeli officers said, 'Nazareth is a Holy City, the world is watching us and you are not going to be victims here.'[3] The first military governor to be appointed for Nazareth was determined to abide by this promise and when the Israeli High Command, a few days later, ordered him to evacuate the population he refused and was immediately relieved of his command. Before leaving he managed to persuade his successor to promise on his word of honour not to harm or displace the Arab population and, fortunately for Nazareth, the promise was kept. Nazareth remains an Arab town to this day.

Many people fled to Nazareth from surrounding towns and villages which had been captured and destroyed, so that the population, which had been 14,000 in 1948, was 40,000 by 1955. At first the refugees were housed in convents and schools and then, as the fighting came to an end, a few were able to return and found their homes intact and unoccupied. The majority, however, had lost everything and had to start a new life in Nazareth living where they could but at least they felt they were still among Palestinians.

The Nakbha (the Catastrophe) had a profound effect on all Palestinians, including those who found themselves part of the new state of Israel. Whole lives had been turned upside down, families had been split by hostile borders, many had been killed, a proud Arab nation had been conquered and their Arab brethren had not been able to help them. They were under military occupation and they could not go anywhere without a permit, which had to be renewed daily. They had no leaders to speak for them since most of the educated and well-to-do had left before the fighting actually started, thinking, of course, like everybody else, that they would shortly return. Nazareth was fortunate in having the EMMS Hospital and some local doctors, two of whom had managed to return from Lebanon after the armistice. I remember that the schools were staffed by the erstwhile senior pupils who, as soon as they graduated from secondary school, were recruited as teachers.

I realise now that the people were in a state of shock. They were completely preoccupied in finding a way to survive economically and emotionally, in trying to come to terms with the new, strange situation in which they found themselves. They did not talk much about their experiences, the suffering was too close and also they had to learn to live under a military authority. They learned to trust no-one.

The Nazareth Hospital had 100 beds under the care of just three doctors, so we had to be prepared to deal with anything that came along. I had been trained as a paediatrician but was soon shown how to manage midwifery cases, give anaesthetics and perform simple operations (as well as how to share the Gospel stories with the patients). Benefitting from weekly language lessons, I slowly acquired a working knowledge of Arabic which made things easier and more interesting.

Life was hard and people were traumatized by what had happened to them. Living under occupation is not easy but slowly the Palestinians came to terms with their new situation. They seemed noisy, very demanding and argumentative. They always knew better than I did about how their disease should be managed! Probably this side of their character was accentuated by their suffering. They could not shout at the occupying powers so they shouted at me — not because I was British, and therefore indirectly responsible for the Balfour Declaration, but because they looked on what they termed the 'English' Hospital as their property. In 1967, people from the Old City of Jerusalem who had been involved in a bus accident were brought to the hospital. I remember being very struck by their attitude because instead of all shouting at once and demanding my immediate attention for their wounds, they said, 'Attend to that man first, he is in a worse condition than me.' At that time, so soon after the 1967 war, they had not yet had the experience of living under Israeli occupation.

The only work available — either in the kibbutzim or as casual labourers in Haifa — involved the daily struggle of getting a permit to travel, then the likelihood of being picked off the bus and being forced to wait at the side of the road for another which might or might not appear. Workers arose at 4 am, got the bus at 4.30 am and reached Haifa to start work at 6 am. After a 12-hour shift they would return home at 8 pm, earning the equivalent of £5 per day.

As a result of the poverty there were many sick children in the hospital — one day I counted two babies in each cot. We had many newborn infants admitted with tetanus (lockjaw) as the local custom was to put cow dung on the umbilical stump after cutting the cord with whatever implement happened to be handy. Most of these babies did not survive but one did and his father brought him back to see us. We had argued fiercely as the father had wanted to take him home to die but I had won and the father bore me no grudge. As the years went by this problem disappeared as mothers came to the hospital to deliver their babies. The Israeli government introduced a national insurance scheme for all maternity cases, both Jewish and Arab, paying the hospital and the mother for a confinement.

The Palestinian custom of cooking with stoves or over an open fire meant that burns were all too common. The local practice, that had evolved from limited access to medical help was to apply coffee grounds, a relatively harmless step and infinitely better than the alternative remedy of applying toothpaste which was very difficult to remove. We instituted the 'open treatment' for burns, for the inpatients, which consisted of the application of a paint, such as gentian violet, without any bandages. One day, I came to see a patient in the children's ward with burns on his bottom. The mother, or some other relative, always stayed with the child. He had asked his mother to 'dry up his wounds' so she had applied coffee grounds very liberally. An open burn is of course very painful, as the air impinges on the exposed nerve endings so the mothers' first aid treatments were certainly effective in easing the pain and were relatively sterile. We encouraged them to apply only a piece of clean cloth until they could reach the hospital.

The babies were still being swaddled very tightly with gaily-embroidered bands. Obviously it is much easier to carry a swaddled baby in one's arms, when one is carrying a large basket on one's head. The problem in this was that by forcibly extending the baby's legs, in order to make them grow straight, all too often the hip joints were dislocated and congenital dislocation of the hip was very common. We slowly educated the mothers and grandmothers to understand that they were unwittingly causing damage and that to put a big napkin between the legs and leggings was much better (then the baby could be wrapped up so that he or she was easy to carry).

The poverty also meant that heating of houses was nonexistent and, in the winter, temperatures in and around Nazareth could fall to zero so hypothermia was another major problem. Mothers of course knew that they must keep their babies warm but they would pile on layer after layer of cheap synthetic garments so that the baby could not move, got colder and colder and eventually froze. The appearance of hypothermic babies is very deceptive as they have bright pink cheeks. Again we had to explain that fewer looser-fitting garments, preferably of wool, inside which the baby could move and kick, were far better.

Even in 1955 I could write 'village teaching is the real essential. Perhaps we can save a few children in the hospital but if we could prevent the illness we could save hundreds'. It was to be twenty years before I could devote myself to preventive medicine.

Because the Arab women wanted and sometimes even demanded a woman doctor I was always more than welcome. I realised that some of the women did not always look upon me as a 'proper doctor', but as a glorified midwife. This could be an advantage. If I sat with them in the labour room because I was concerned about them and wanted to keep an eye on them they were not worried. However, if they themselves felt things were moving too slowly they would say to me, 'Should you not call the doctor now?'

We were always free to talk about the Christian faith as the hospital is known throughout a large part of the Middle East as a Christian establishment, although perhaps seventy per cent of the patients were Muslims. We always prayed for patients in the theatre before operating. They would say to me, as I prepared to give them their anaesthetic, 'Are you not going to pray for me?' On Sundays we were able to worship in one of the many churches in Nazareth and share in fellowship there with the Christians.

1   (Copyright ©1973, 1978, 1984 by International Bible Society. Used by permission of Hodder & Stoughton Ltd. All rights reserved.)
2   Michael Palumbo, *The Palestinian Catastrophe* (Faber & Faber, London, 1987, p. 123)
3   Palumbo, *The Palestinian Catastrophe*, p. 123

5

THE SIXTIES AND THE SIX DAY WAR

'Were half the power that fills the world with terror
Were half the wealth bestowed on camps and courts
Given to redeem the human mind from error
There were no need of arsenals or forts.'

Henry Wadsworth Longfellow[1]

Life for the Palestinians in Israel, within what came to be known as the Green Line — the 1949 armistice line between Israel and Jordan — slowly changed and, it must be admitted, materially it changed for the better. There was more money and, so long as Arabs did not raise their voices against the regime, they could go about their daily business, but woe betide any voice of dissent. In the 1960s the Arabs were beginning to gain entrance to the universities in Israel. Even in the 1990s although they make up eighteen per cent of the population of Israel they represent only six per cent of the student body. It is often students who speak out against injustices — Arab students were no exception and therefore fell foul of the security services. We knew the government had files on all of us and that mail was censored so we just learned to be careful.

One of the most important parts of the work of the hospital had always been the training of nurses. In 1955 we ran a two-year course for practical nurses. We taught in English and the government allowed our students to sit the government examination in English. In 1963 we began to train these practical nurses in a sixteen-month practical midwifery course, still in English and again recognised by the government.

The maternity department was becoming increasingly busy, the Arab birth rate being one of the highest in the world (in 1965 we had 3,310 deliveries). It was then that I decided to start a family planning clinic. Many mothers just could not cope with another baby and would ask me to terminate their pregnancy. I knew I must be able to offer a better alternative than a termination so we began to offer family planning advice. We did not advertise, the news just spread by word of mouth and our clientele grew. It is a well-known fact that as the standard of living rises and the infant mortality rate falls and women become more educated, they themselves make the decision to limit their families.

Some years later, when I was working in a government family planning clinic, we had an unexpected visit from an official of the International Planned Parenthood Federation. He had been sent to investigate a bogus claim by the Arab League that the Israeli government was forcing Arab women to be sterilised because their birth rate was far higher than the Jewish. I advised the official to ask the waiting women himself, 'Why did you come to the clinic, who told you to come?' Each one answered, 'My neighbour told me about it,' or 'My husband told me to come,' or 'I decided myself that I wanted a rest.' There were other contributory factors such as the fact that in the past a woman might have twelve children but only six survived so she needed to have a big family. When the Palestinians had their own land they needed a lot of children to work the land but so few of them now had any land to farm, this was no longer a necessity. The village of Ibilin still has some land and I did not get very far in suggesting to the local people that family spacing might be a good idea!

Children in Arab families are much beloved and many women saw their role in life solely as bearers of children and they would come to me, when the youngest was three or four for 'treatment for children', and I would say, 'But you already have six or seven', or whatever it was and they would say, 'But my hands are empty'. Large extended families are a great protection against child abuse. I never saw a 'battered baby'— there was always an older sibling to carry the crying baby outdoors and there were no locked doors behind which a child could be seriously beaten. Wives did sometimes suffer but again the close family relationships helped — 'if you maltreat your wife (my sister) then I will divorce my wife (your sister).'

Illegitimate pregnancies were always a nightmare since the woman's life would certainly not be spared if her brothers or father found out — family honour rested heavily upon the woman being faithful to her husband. The man concerned was not considered to have been responsible — he must have been seduced — so he got off scot-free. We had to keep the woman hidden and give the baby a false name until she could go home and we could find a home for the baby. The local Arab social workers were a tremendous support to me and would even take the girls into their own homes for safety. According to Israeli law babies can only be adopted by couples of the same religion (this was to prevent Jewish babies being adopted by Gentiles). Muslims did not recognise the existence of illegitimate babies because they believed that the mother and the baby should have been killed, so the only people who could legally adopt Arab babies were Christian Arabs or foreigners. The Jewish social worker from Haifa was a realist. When I explained our problem, as most of the babies up for adoption were of Muslim mothers we worked out a solution. If the father's religion was unknown to the mother, we asked her to sign a paper stating that she did not want her child and then we christened the baby. The Jews saw baptism as the sign and proof of Christianity so now the baby could be legally adopted by a Christian couple. We found homes for most of them this way.

Before the days of artificial insemination, infertility was another problem and usually ended in divorce or the taking of a second wife. The man was not willing to accept that he might be responsible. If the first wife did not want a divorce — which would involve her returning to her father's house — she would, if she was wise, look around for someone with whom she felt could share her house, preferably a woman who already had a child. She would then suggest this woman to her husband and then the first wife still retained her place in the home and helped the second wife in the upbringing of her children. Often it worked out quite well for everybody concerned.

One Muslim couple asked me to help them in a most ingenious scheme. The wife announced that she was pregnant, and, wearing voluminous garments nobody could deny it. Then they went to the social worker and asked if they could adopt the next illegitimate baby to be born. We sometimes admitted mothers with their newborn babies within twenty-four hours of a home delivery, if they had not been able to reach the hospital in time, so, at the appropriate time, I admitted the mother with the baby. The baby was actually one month old — big for a 'newborn' and my Swiss nursery nurse had been suspicious she told me months later, but all that the Arab nurses were worried about was that the mother refused to breast feed. I told them to give the baby a bottle as the mother was very 'fussy' and they accepted that explanation. Mother and son went home, absolutely delighted.

At the same time war clouds were gathering on the horizon and 1967 was a momentous year for the Arab world. On 6 June Israel attacked Egypt's airfields, in a pre-emptive strike, and destroyed the entire air force in minutes. Jordan came into the war as she had just signed a defence treaty with Egypt, but was swiftly defeated. This lightning military victory for Israel — in which she captured the West Bank of the Jordan, Jerusalem, the Gaza Strip and the Golan Heights — left the Arab world devastated militarily, strategically, geographically and emotionally. The Palestinian refugees from 1948 who had been living in the camps on the West Bank of the Jordan, fled across the Jordan River and were napalmed from the air. Others fled north and south thus increasing the numbers of refugees in Jordan, Lebanon, Syria and Gaza. In Nazareth, we were spared any direct effects of the fighting, except for a complete blackout and two air raid warnings. Work continued uninterrupted.

Israel, too, was knocked sideways by her success. She seemed to have little or no idea about how to deal with her newly acquired territories, except for Jerusalem, and she wasted no time in annexing the whole of it and declaring it the 'eternal capital of Israel'. The rest of her conquests became the 'Occupied Territories', and the 1.3 million Palestinians became a subject people without rights. By the 1949 Fourth Geneva Convention on Occupation, when a people are occupied, a Protecting Power must be appointed. Unfortunately, in 1967 this was not done.

The UN passed Resolution 242 on 22 November 1967 which demanded that Israeli forces withdraw from territories occupied in the recent conflict and that there must be respect for the rights of all Middle Eastern states to live in peace within secure and recognised borders. The wording is hopelessly 'woolly' and is open to different interpretations. Israel defines 'territories' in her own terms — not, as 'all territories' just *some* of them, as demonstrated when she handed back the Sinai to Egypt. The wording 'All Middle Eastern states' includes Israel, so confirms Israel's right to exist on the land of Palestine, so the Resolution was rejected by Syria, Iraq and of course by the Palestinians. Egypt and Jordan meant to find a diplomatic rather than a military solution (following their devastating defeat) so they secretly accepted 242.

As a result, nothing happened. No handing back of territory, no return home of refugees and increasingly draconian measures were employed to control the Occupied Territories.

We, who lived inside the Green Line, now had the opportunity of visiting the West Bank and the Old City of Jerusalem and at first there was a certain amount of euphoria as people were able to meet relatives they had not seen for twenty years. In the winter of 1968 I studied Arabic in Bethlehem. Talking to people there I sensed a deep fear of the Israelis, not only because of their military might and US support, but also because the Arabs felt that they would never be able to compete with the Jews in any sphere of life. This engendered a terrible hopelessness and despair.

I tried introducing an Arab friend of mine from Nazareth to a Jewish friend in Haifa. They were both very happy to meet each other but, as soon as the conversation came around to the crucial issues of the day, a kind of barrier went up. Both tried to justify their side's actions and neither side wanted to listen to the other. The only thing they had in common was genuine sympathy for the mothers of those who had been killed in the war.

It is not anti-semitism that causes this divide. Arabs and Jews are both Semites, both children of Abraham, blood brothers. Palestinians will always tell you, 'We don't hate the Jews, we hate Zionism and the policies of the Israeli government'.

The Palestinians as a people now had to rethink their position too. They were as devastated as the rest of the Arab world by the 1967 defeat and realised that it was useless to rely on the other Arab states to regain their land for them. From now on, they must depend on their own efforts. Mounting Palestinian frustration and the determination of the Arab states to control that frustration had led to the creation of the Palestine Liberation Organisation (PLO) in 1964 in Egypt under the aegis of President Nasser. Control of the PLO, however, slipped out of the hands of the Arab governments, with the rise of the guerilla movements in the mid-1960s. Of these, by far the most important was the Palestine Liberation Movement, known by its Arabic acronym, Fatah (meaning 'victory'). It was founded in the late 1950s by Yasser Arafat, Khalil Wazir, Khalid al-Hassan and Salah Khalaf and its platform was that Palestine can only be liberated by a popular movement

taking place on Palestinian soil. It does not approve of, or participate in, attacks on Israeli or Jewish targets in third countries. The
actions of other guerilla groups in this regard have been a serious
embarrassment to Fatah.

The largest and most enduring of these other guerilla groups
which do not share Fatah's pragmatic approach are the Popular
Front for the Liberation of Palestine (PFLP), which is Marxist in
ideology and led by Dr George Habash, a Greek Orthodox Christian, and the Democratic Front for the Liberation of Palestine,
(DFLP), also led by a Greek Orthodox Christian, Naif Hawatmeh
and which is ideologically even further 'left'.

The PLO's leading secular ideological groups have sprung from
the Greek Orthodox Church and the inter-Arab Socialist parties,
namely the Ba'ath (renaissance) and the Syrian National Socialist
Party. Perhaps this reflects the search of Arab Christians for an
ideology that will erase the implicit disadvantage of Christians in
a predominantly Muslim world. A Palestinian Christian doctor
said to me, after the defeat of 1967, 'We Christians cannot accept
defeat now, today — the Muslims are prepared to wait for Palestine for years, for decades if necessary'.

The most ruthless, dangerous and therefore the most notorious guerilla group is that of Abu Nidal which has been highly
successful in compromising PLO chances of getting a hearing in-
ternationally or of discussing a pragmatic settlement.

By 1969 the prestige of Fatah enabled its leader Yasser Arafat
to become Chairman of the PLO Executive. This was the birth of
the PLO as we know it today. Arafat has always tried to keep the
smaller groups 'within the fold', believing that they are safer 'inside' rather than in opposition. This policy also meant that the
different Arab countries which sponsored the different groups,
also gave their indirect support to the PLO.

A guerilla organisation requires a base from which to operate,
the PLO had no base of its own, no land, hence its continuing need
of other Arab countries. At first the PLO used Jordan, until it fell
foul of the Jordanian army and threatened the stability and sovereignty of the Hashemite kingdom. It was almost becoming 'a state
within a state' and was brutally suppressed and driven out of Jordan in September 1970. Likewise when the PLO moved to Lebanon there were clashes between the Christian paramilitary groups
and the Palestinians from the 1970s through to the 1990s.

The PLO is, however, far more than a political and military structure. In Lebanon, from 1969 onwards, it developed social and educational services in the camps and the slum areas of Beirut which helped the Lebanese as well as the Palestinian refugees. Kindergartens catered for hundreds of children and enabled their mothers to work. The PLO also created the first genuinely popular health service in Lebanon — the Palestine Red Crescent Society (PRCS), which was affiliated to the International Red Cross. Its network of clinics and hospitals provided free care, regardless of religion or nationality. In the south some of its services were used more by the Lebanese than the Palestinians. But all these social and other services which had given the camp populations a sense of dignity and purpose, were deliberately smashed by Israel when it invaded Lebanon in 1982. Only a shadow of the former organization still continues to operate in Lebanon.

1 'The Arsenal At Springfield', *The Golden Treasury* (Oxford University Press, Oxford, 1940, p. 340)

6

THE SEVENTIES
AND THE YOM KIPPUR WAR

*'I remember in the most bitter days of the Holocaust somebody
asked me, "What revenge can there be?" and I replied, "We will
build something of such moral value, something of such human
decency and dignity that all the people who throughout the ages
hated and persecuted us will come to our doors to learn from us.'*

Prime Minister Golda Meir's Jewish New Year message
which appeared in the Jerusalem Post, 1971.

Sadly, the dispossessed Palestinians were not to be treated with
decency and dignity under Golda Meir's government.

The 1970s dawned with a continuation of the state of 'no peace,
no war' in the Middle East. President Sadat of Egypt had been
stalling for so long about resolving this state that the Israelis were
beginning to think he was bluffing. So, when the Egyptian army
eventually struck on 13 October 1973 (the Jewish Day of Atone-
ment), they had the great advantage of the element of surprise.
They crossed the Suez Canal and the Syrian army advanced into
Israel. The Israel Defence Force (IDF) took seventy-two hours to
mobilise. The Egyptians however were not able to consolidate
their gains and the Israeli army soon pushed the Syrians back.
The rest of the Arab world did respond this time, with the 'oil
weapon'. The Organisation of Petroleum Exporting Countries
declared it would cut oil production to five per cent a month until
Israel withdrew from all occupied Arab territories. Saudi Arabia
reduced production by ten per cent and enforced a total oil em-
bargo on the US and the Netherlands. The rich industrial West,
so dependent on oil, was appalled and the US and the Soviet Union worked hard to get a cease-fire. The war came to an end after
seventeen days of fighting. Both sides suffered heavy losses of
men and equipment. Israel was 'victorious', but the Arabs were
now in a better position. They had proved that their armed forces
could fight courageously and that their leaders could be as skilful

as the Israelis and, by their use of the 'oil weapon', they had been able to hurt the 'mighty West'.

I was actually on leave in Scotland that October and saw the outbreak of the war on TV. I was fortunate to be able to get back to Nazareth thirty-six hours later and found the hospital empty. It soon became very busy as the Israeli hospitals were then taking only military casualties, so many Arabs came to us. Patients were usually able to go to the hospital of their choice, regardless of race or religion.

The PLO now had to decide how to react to the new postwar situation. Arafat reached the conclusion that Palestinian demands should be scaled down to the creation of a small state of Palestine out of the West Bank and the Gaza Strip, that is the Occupied Territories. Other groups in the PLO, however, refused to abandon the goal of making the whole of pre-1948 Palestine a democratic nonsectarian state for Arabs and Jews. Again great pressure was placed on the PLO to accept UN Resolution 242. This, however, made no mention of the Palestinian refugees, except in a cursory reference to the need for a just settlement of the 'refugee problem' — the Palestinians were a 'problem' not a 'people' with rights.

Throughout the 1970s Israel was relentlessly pursuing its policy of setting up settlements in the Occupied Territories while continuing to expropriate Arab land within the Green Line. In 1950 Israel had passed 'the law of Absentees', legitimizing the transfer of land not only from those Arabs driven out but also from those displaced internally — the Arabs who remained in Israel lost forty per cent of their land. Israel also confiscated *Waqf* (Islamic) property — thousands of acres of land as well as houses, businesses and shops — but not actual mosques. To be able to keep their land the Israeli Arabs were required to produce 'proof of ownership' in the form of certificates from the British Mandatory Authority. In 1989 a resident in Jabaaliya camp in Gaza showed me the title deeds to his property in Ashkelon, and they were entitled 'Government of Palestine'. The British had not been able to complete this documentation before the end of the Mandate. They had concentrated on areas which were then under dispute between Arabs and Jews and had left the purely Arab areas to be dealt with later since they were perceived as non-urgent at the time. In the absence of documents Israel simply declared the land to be state land and handed it over to the Jewish Agency. Israel also used an old Ottoman law which allowed for the seizure of land which had gone out of cultivation for three years and a boundary law which used the distance the human voice carried to define it. Other areas were cordoned off for 'security reasons'.

30 March1976 became known as Land Day. The people of Galilee were becoming desperate, as they saw more and more of their lands being expropriated by the government. They would be offered a ridiculously low price, far less than the value, and if they refused the land was expropriated anyway. A peaceful demonstration against this policy was planned, but the army opened fire on the demonstrators and six Arabs were killed.

Life in Nazareth was, however, improving in some ways. The Arabs within the Green Line have Israeli passports but these are inscribed 'Citizen of Israel, nationality Arab'. Only Jews can be nationals of Israel. Israeli Arabs, men and women, have the right to vote but a specifically Arab party is forbidden. The Progressive List for Peace, which was an Arab attempt in the 1990s to set up their own Arab party, came to nothing as it would have signified a change in the Israeli concept of what Israel is — a Jewish state. Arabs must support one of the Jewish parties if they wish to vote within the parliamentary system. Many of those who accept the state of Israel but want an equal share in it, join the Communist Party, Rakah, which is non-Zionist but loyal to the idea of an Israeli state. In the 1977 election there was a major swing to the Communist Party among the Arabs. Nazareth elected a Communist mayor, Tawfik Ziyyad, a well-known Palestinian poet, tragically killed in 1994 in a motor crash as he was returning from a visit to Chairman Arafat in Jericho. The Communists, many of them Christian Arabs, were really more like Nationalists than Soviet Communists. I had a vote because I was a permanent resident and many of us voted for the Communist Party in the local elections as they were not as corrupt as the other parties.

The villages around Nazareth did not enjoy the same standard of living as the city dwellers, some of them still had no paved access road, only a mud track which became impassable in the winter. One year there was an epidemic of typhoid fever in one such village and the people could not get out for treatment so we had to evacuate them on the backs of donkeys. A few years later another village sent an SOS to the medical officer of health in Nazareth for medical help. The medical officer approached the Israeli Army who provided a helicopter and we provided the personnel from the hospital. It was fascinating to be flying so low over Galilee. When we landed, the *Muktar* (the headman of the village) called all the would-be patients to the school. I examined at least forty children and prescribed appropriate medicines but not one was really ill enough to warrant transfer to hospital. An army officer asked me on our return, 'Was your journey really necessary?' and I replied, 'It was for the people concerned'. The village got a paved road by the next winter!

Gradually all the villages were supplied with running water and electricity. One day in the clinic, in exasperation at the noise made by the seventy or eighty women waiting to be seen, I said, 'Must you make all this noise?' They replied, 'Now that we have water in our houses we no longer gather at the village well to meet our friends and to exchange the gossip of the village so we have to meet here in the clinic!' The coming of the water was a mixed blessing!

On 5 September 1978 President Sadat of Egypt, Prime Minister Begin of Israel and President Carter of the US held an extraordinary meeting at which the famous Camp David Accords were signed. They comprised two agreements, namely to provide a framework for peace in the Middle East to deal with the Palestinian question, and a framework for peace with Egypt.

The latter was fairly straightforward, providing for the restoration of Egyptian sovereignty over its territory and normalization of relations between the two countries. On 26 March 1979 a peace treaty was signed in Washington. Israel dismantled the settlements in the Sinai, against great opposition from the settlers (although they received large sums in compensation), and returned the oilfields to Egypt. The framework for the Palestinian question was, from the beginning, only a pious hope. Israel had no intention of relinquishing control over any of the Occupied Territories although it had been made clear in the Accords that they should set up an interim local self-governing authority which would, after five years, provide full autonomy for the inhabitants. The PLO was the sole representative of the Palestinians and Israel refused to recognise it, let alone talk to it, so nothing happened. President Sadat had, in fact, committed the cardinal sin in Arab eyes, he had signed a separate peace treaty with Israel.

October 1979 saw the award of the Nobel Peace Prize jointly to President Sadat and Prime Minister Menachem Begin, erstwhile leader of the Irgun which had perpetrated the Deir Yassin massacre.

President Sadat's Peace Treaty with Israel enabled Israel to invade Lebanon in 1982, as her southern border with Egypt had been made secure.

7

A CHANGE OF DIRECTION

'With all these witnesses to faith around me like a cloud, I must run with resolution the race for which I am entered.'

Hebrews 12.1, New English Bible[1]

I watched the changes that more education and better economic conditions brought to the women. They were not all good. For instance the decline in breast feeding meant that the incidence of gastroenteritis in Arab babies did not drop, although, with the good care provided in Israeli hospitals as well as in ours, the mortality rate fell.

I was becoming increasingly interested in primary child health care so, in 1976, after twenty years of working in the Nazareth Hospital, I was granted a year's sabbatical leave and went off to India. There I found villages where no children had been hospitalized for gastroenteritis for two years and I thought, surely the hospitals in Israel every summer should not be filled with our Arab babies with gastroenteritis. I had a growing realisation that Christian medical witness should not be confined within the walls of a hospital but should be lived in the community. So I decided to return to Nazareth and to leave the hospital. I rented an apartment nearby and joined the Ministry of Health as a district medical officer and was assigned some of the villages near Nazareth. I worked hard with the Ministry of Health nurses, who were Arabic-speaking Jews who had volunteered to work in the Arab sector, and also some of the Arabs who had trained in our hospital.

In 1982 I was given the opportunity to take on the job of *Kopat Holim* (the Sick Fund) paediatrician in one of the villages in which I was working. All the children whose parents had Sick Fund insurance, about eighty-one per cent, came under my care. Now I found I had a much more receptive audience. But still the babies fell ill and had to be hospitalized and the mother could not accept that she or anybody else could do anything to prevent it. She thought it was 'normal' because the baby was teething or a snake had spat on the food and ultimately it was the will of God.

In 1981 a number of health professionals, myself included, founded the government-registered Galilee Society for Health Research and Service (GSHRS), a non-profit making organization, to improve the health of the rural communities in Galilee. In 1983 we were able to initiate a two-year model community health education programme (funded by the US Ford Foundation) in Kufr Manda, a village of about 6,600 people. We concentrated on the prevention of diarrhoea because it was so common and could be tackled through health education. We also tested the acceptability and effectiveness of oral rehydration therapy — used worldwide, but frowned upon in Israel. It took another six years before we were able to convince the Israeli paediatricians to use it and to get its use authorized by the Ministry of Health.

We were able to find four people from the village to train as community health educators and sent them for an eight-month training course, run by the Catholic Relief Services in Nablus on the West Bank. These students sometimes found it difficult to travel from within the Green Line to the West Bank, because of curfews but they persevered and later started work in the village. They organised 'neighbourhood coffee mornings' and held classes on such diverse subjects as breast feeding and the best way of dealing with garbage to reduce the fly population! We found that the community leaders, heads of the families, the imam of the mosque, the local elected village council, teachers, as well as the people themselves, were interested and anxious to improve the health of their village. The imam preached on health-related subjects in his Friday sermon, the village council provided covered garbage cans for each household and relocated the garbage dump well away from the village. We gave health lectures in the school, targeting the teenage girls since they play such an important role in the home, looking after younger siblings and sharing the household chores as well as being the mothers of the future.

The community health educators themselves set a good example — in breast feeding their own babies and ignoring advice from neighbours and mothers-in-law. One of them was breast feeding and told me that she had declined all the bottles offered to her and was teaching the other mothers in the ward to do the same.

They were always coming up with good ideas and the work goes on. The village is hardly recognisable now in the 1990s. I always had to keep reminding myself that people mattered more than the 'project'. I would get mad when I saw a child sick with something preventable, but I had to let the mother understand that I was not so mad with her as with the disease and only because I longed for her child to be well just as she did.

1   (*New English Bible* © Oxford University Press and Cambridge University Press 1961, 1970)

8

LIFE IN LEBANON

The Arabs are incapable of founding an empire unless they are imbued with religious enthusiasm by a prophet or a saint.

Words attributed to Ibn Khaldun, fourteenth-century Arab historian.[1]

In 1920 France was given the Mandate for Syria and Lebanon and proceeded to alter the borders, to truncate Syria and to make a 'Greater Lebanon' to their liking, with Mount Lebanon, the Bekaa valley, Akka in the north, Tripoli, Beirut, Tyre and Sidon. A new nation was thus created, at the behest of the Christian Maronites, with artificial borders which had no basis in history. It was a miscalculation on the part of the Maronites, in one way, because they thus got a large Muslim majority.

From the beginning of history Syria has been recognised as a single geographical entity. At the end of the First World War President Wilson of the US set up the King Crane Commission which visited the area and interviewed many people, of which only sixteen per cent asked for a French Mandate, most people preferring the US or Britain! Eighty per cent of the petitions submitted called for a united Syria. The Commission recommended that, 'The unity of Syria be preserved, in accordance with the earnest petition of the great majority of the people of Syria.'[2] These recommendations were totally ignored, and most of today's problems, particularly the Israel-Palestine and the Lebanese conflict, can be traced back to the decision to divide 'the spoils of war' between Britain and France.

In 1941, the non-Vichy government which did not collaborate with Nazi Germany — the Free French — promised Lebanon and Syria their sovereignty and independence, but were slow to act. Khouri Bishara (a Maronite) was elected to the Presidency in 1943 and he and the Sunni Muslim Prime Minister, Riad al Sulh, together worked out the National Pact which, although unwritten, became the bedrock of Lebanese political life until the collapse of authority in 1975 with the outbreak of civil war.

The National Pact reserves governmental posts for different religions — the president must be a Maronite Christian, the prime minister a Sunni Muslim and the president of the Chamber of Deputies a Shi'ite Muslim. The other posts in government and seats in the Chamber of Deputies reflect the composition of Lebanese society on a crude ratio of six Christians to five Muslims.

In practice it formalised and hardened the need for sectarian balance, making it virtually impossible to move away from a political life which was based on religious divides.

The National Pact was based on the last census which was taken in 1932 and showed fifty-two per cent Christian and forty-eight per cent Muslim. (Nobody has dared to take another since!) The population has increased from one million to perhaps three-and-a-half million and the higher birth rate among the Muslims means that the balance has changed. It therefore has become inevitable that those who feel disadvantaged by what has become a myth are now raising their voices for a 'fairer share of the cake'.

' Go up to Lebanon, and cry out.'

Jeremiah 22.20 (New International Version of the Holy Bible)[3]

It was in the late 1970s that I came to know something about Lebanon. In 1978 the Israel Defence Force had invaded Lebanon for the first time, and occupied the country as far north as the Litani River. However, they withdrew a few weeks later as the United Nations Interim Force in Lebanon (UNIFIL) took up its position in south Lebanon and Israel handed over the remaining enclave of the occupied area to its surrogate army, led by the renegade Lebanese Major Hadad, an area which he later proclaimed 'Free Lebanon', but which Israel calls 'The Security Zone'. In June 1982 Israel launched its second massive invasion. Up until then Lebanon had been, for me, just the country to the north of Israel, whose picturesque little villages we could see as we drove along the northern border. From now on, however, Lebanon was seldom out of the news and came to play a very significant part in my life.

Lebanon is Israel's northern neighbour, and the home of 250,000 Palestinian refugees, the vast majority of whom are the descendants of those who fled from their villages in Galilee in 1948. Lebanon has been described as 'a collection of traditional communities, bound by the mutual understanding that other communities cannot be trusted.'[4] It is so small that it could fit into one quarter of Switzerland and is, basically, a country formed of minorities. It is the conflicting aspirations and fears of these different components of Lebanese society confined in a small and rapidly urbanizing area which lie at the heart of Lebanon's civil war. 'The non-Lebanese ingredients to the conflict, the Syrian, Israeli and Palestinian-armed presence and the interference of the two superpowers have certainly exacerbated the conflict but none of them started it. Civil conflict feeds on internal divisions and had these not existed the Lebanese would undoubtedly have closed ranks against their neighbours'.[5]

Throughout the Middle East the bonds of loyalty are grounded in kinship and religion. Outside family loyalties, which direct so much daily life, the Lebanese belong, first and foremost, to their religious confession. Lebanon is called a confessional state because the Ottomans introduced the religious or confessional principle into government. Like kinship, it is a bond of loyalty that is traced back over centuries, and which, under the 400-year rule of the Ottomans, was institutionalized in the 'millet' system. All Ottoman citizens were defined according to their religion, and sect within that religion, so that people felt their identity to be essentially religious.

Lebanon's religious communities can be broadly divided into Christian and Muslim. The Christian communities date from the earliest days of the Church and the main ones are Greek (or Arab) Orthodox which has its seat in Antioch, Turkey; the Greek Catholic Church, a splinter from the Orthodox — which came into union with Rome in the eighteenth century — retains its oriental rites and customs; the Maronite Church which is in union with Rome but is of different origin, is rooted in its Monothelite doctrine.

Monothelitism arose in the seventh century and claimed that in Christ there is but one will. In AD 648 the first Lateran Council condemned Monothelitism and proclaimed 'as in Christ there are two natures, human and divine, so there are two wills and two energies in perfect harmony. As the Gospel tells us in the Garden of Gethsemane Jesus said, not My will but Thine be done. A Christ without a human will would not be perfect man nor a true mediator — He would be wanting in that faculty which in man has been the instrument of sin and needs redemption.'[6] The Maronites were persecuted for the 'heresy' of monothelitism by the Orthodox Byzantine Church and then suffered under the conquering Muslim armies, so they retreated from northern Syria into the northern fastness of Mount Lebanon. In 1216 they abandoned the Monothelite heresy and established relations with Rome but only entered into formal union with the Holy See in 1736. They take their name, either from a Syrian hermit called St Maron or from John Maron their first Patriach.

Until the nineteenth century the Maronites remained confined to Mount Lebanon and it was there that they established their own feudal structure but developed a deep sense of affinity with Christian Europe, particularly with France. Maronites to this day use French as their first language and even deny being Arabs, saying that they are Phoenicians. They feel themselves to be European, not part of the Arab world, and are seen in this way by the rest of Lebanon. They have lived in their mountains for thirteen centuries and Lebanon is the only country where they have an important presence. This has given them a different outlook from the Druze, Greek Catholic or Greek Orthodox who are spread over other countries. The Maronites — regarding themselves as 'special' in terms of their religion — have played and continue to play a very significant role in Lebanon.

Other Christian communities include very small Eastern churches. There are also Roman Catholics and Protestants, the result of missionary work over the past 200 years and which therefore make them tend to look to the West for their cultural and political affinities.

The Christian world tends to lump all Muslims together into the 'Muslim World', but Islam, too, is riven with different traditions and tensions based on historical experience. The Sunni community forms the 'Muslim Establishment' as Sunni Islam was the official religion of the Ottoman Empire and this gave the Sunnis an implicitly superior status to their co-religionists and members of other faiths.

The Shi'ites are the followers of Ali, the Prophet Muhammad's son-in-law. They lost in the succession struggle, on the death of the Prophet, but have remained faithful to Ali. They have, traditionally, been the poorest and most exploited, politically the least-represented and socially the least-educated group in Lebanon. They are the predominant sect living in the south of Lebanon. It is also important to remember that for centuries Shi'ism has been the established faith of Iran.

A third Islamic sect, although, to Orthodox Muslims, they are heretics, are the Druze. Historically they spring from the claim of the Fatimid Caliph of Egypt, al Hakim (AD 996-1020), to be the 'emanation of God in His unity'. This teaching was brutally suppressed in Egypt, on al Hakim's 'disappearance' in 1020, but some of his disciples escaped to the mountains of Lebanon and taught the new doctrine there, founding a sect named after an early follower of al Hakim, called Darazi. The actual tenets of their religion are known only to the 'initiated' and they remain a very tight-knit community never marrying 'out'. I came to know them well when I worked in Israel as there are several Druze villages near the Lebanese border. The Druze women absolutely refuse to see a male doctor, preferring even to die, so I would always be called to see and treat them. In Lebanon they are much freer and there only the elderly women wear the traditional long black dress and white headscarf. The older men wear baggy black trousers and white skull cap. One of their beliefs is in the 'transmigration of souls'. A Druze friend in Lebanon named his second son after a brother killed in the war. He told me that although he was delighted with his new son he was at the same time sad that somebody else must have lost a son.

The Druze living within Israel are loyal citizens of the state, serve in the Israeli army and are not now even considered a minority as are other Arabs. They practice the doctrine of *taqiyya* — the concealment of their beliefs when amongst unbelievers, yet as with all non-Jewish inhabitants they are not Israeli nationals. The Druze living on the Golan Heights — captured from Syria in 1967 — have always refused to take Israeli identity cards. On Mount Lebanon they had their own militia during the Lebanese civil war.

There are two other major communities in Lebanon identified by their immigrant identity rather than their religion and both of them came to Lebanon after 1920. The Armenians — composed of Armenian Orthodox, Catholics and Protestants — arrived as fugitives from the massacres in Anatolia at the end of the nineteenth century. They have always done their best to avoid controversy and to demonstrate their loyalty to Lebanon.

The Palestinians arrived in a massive influx from Palestine in 1948. Some were the bourgeoisie and intellectual elite of Haifa who settled in Beirut and were able to buy citizenship and were easily assimilated into the upper strata of Lebanese society. The majority, however, maybe 104,000, arrived empty-handed believing they would soon be returning home. When this did not happen a few found friends and relatives, as there had always been a lot of coming and going between Palestine and southern Lebanon. The United Nations Relief and Works Agency (UNRWA) was formed in 1949 especially to help the Palestinian refugees in the Occupied Territories, Lebanon, Syria and Jordan. Seventeen camps were set up near Beirut, Tripoli, Sidon and Tyre for the refugees, who became a pool of unskilled labour as well as a source of resentment to their hosts. From 1950 the Lebanese government controlled the camps very strictly with their Deuxieme Bureau but in 1969 following the revolt of camp inhabitants, the Lebanese army and Chairman Arafat drew up the Cairo Agreement, which permitted any Palestinian in Lebanon to participate in the Palestinian revolution — that is in attacks on Israel — while respecting Lebanese sovereignty and not interfering in the country's affairs. The camps then became 'liberated zones' in charge of Palestinian fighters.

1 Ibn Khaldun, *The Muqaddimah* (Routledge & Kegan Paul Ltd, London, 1958, Vol I, p. 305)
2 David Gilmour, *The Fractured Country* (Sphere Books Ltd, London, 1984, p. 63)
3 (Copyright ©1973, 1978, 1984 by International Bible Society. Used by permission of Hodder & Stoughton Ltd. All rights reserved.)
4 Gilmour, *The Fractured Country*, p. 21
5 David McDowall, *The Palestinians* (Minority Rights Publications, London, 1994, p. 7)
6 A R Whitham, *History of the Christian Church* (Rivington, London, 1963, p. 322)

9

LEBANON'S WARS

'The violence you have done to Lebanon
will overwhelm you ...
For you have shed man's blood;
you have destroyed lands and cities
and everyone in them.'

Habakkuk 2.17 (New International Version of the Holy Bible)[1]

The 1982 Israeli invasion of Lebanon changed Lebanon and also changed Israel. In the 1970s, even if it was not obvious at the time, it has since become clear, that Israel wanted to create an upheaval in Lebanon. The Israeli government knew that the best way to do this was to stir up the antagonism between the Maronites and the Arab nationalists, who, more or less, supported the Palestinians. The Maronite's chief objection to the Palestine Resistance Movement (PRM) was that it had become a magnet for a large number of radical Lebanese groups, including the Druze, which wanted to change the political system. The Palestinians did not help by strutting around Beirut, armed and in uniform and by setting up their own roadblocks. Israel exploited the situation to the full, by mounting raids even into Beirut by sea and air, in order to kill Palestinians, and, inevitably, others got killed too. These actions infuriated the Maronites, as they infringed the very sovereignty of Lebanon.

The civil war began in 1975 and it was kept going by extremists. At the beginning the vast majority of all sects had no intention of getting involved. It was a war between a kind of Christian youth movement founded in 1936 called the Phalangists — which by 1958 had become a political party with a strong militia — and an alliance of radicals, Nasserists and Palestinians outside the control of the PLO. Most people wanted nothing to do with the two warring sides and it was only by stages, and against their will that the Lebanese majority and the Palestinians who identified themselves with Arafat and the mainstream Fatah were dragged into the war. Eventually it became what outsiders had always claimed it to be, a sectarian war. At this time extremists began to kill people simply because they belonged to a different sect, when the thugs of one side or another put up barricades to examine the identity cards of passers-by and put to death all those of the opposing religion. Only then did the people of different faiths come to hate each other to an extent that seemed to justify the continuation of the civil war. (Israel was all the time clandestinely supplying the Maronites with arms, and the countries of the Eastern Block supplied everybody else.)

Between Israel's first invasion of 1978, and the second of 1982, Lebanon remained tense and fragmented with sporadic fighting breaking out in different regions. On 17 July 1981, an Israeli air raid on Beirut killed 350 civilians. Frantic diplomatic moves by the US envoy, Philip Habib, brought about a cease-fire, which held. This was not what Israel wanted. Professor Yehoshua Porath, one of Israel's finest historians, was convinced that Israel's decision to invade in 1982 resulted from the fact that the cease-fire had held. He wrote on 25 June 1982, 'Arafat had succeeded in doing the impossible. He managed an indirect agreement, through American mediation, with Israel and even managed to keep it for a whole year ... this was a disaster for Israel. If the PLO agreed upon, and maintained a cease-fire they may in the future agree to a far more far-reaching political settlement and maintain that too.'[2]

The moderation and responsibility which Arafat had been showing were an obvious threat to the expansionist aims of Israel's leaders and for that reason the PLO had to be destroyed.

There were three other significant developments in 1981. The first was Israel's destruction of Iraq's nuclear reactor. Then Syria, which had had a 'peace keeping' force in Lebanon since 1976, at the Lebanese government's request, stationed Sam 3 ground-to-air missiles near Zahleh in Lebanon. These challenged Israel because they jeopardized her ability to carry out reconnaissance and preventive/attrition attacks on the PLO. Finally the growing power of AMAL, a secret Shi'ite commando group, posed an increasing threat to the Palestinians. AMAL was formed in 1974 to defend the south of Lebanon against Israeli attacks. Because the south of Lebanon is predominantly Shi'ite, AMAL was strongest in the south and, at first, supported the PRM against the Israelis and their surrogate South Lebanese Army. Even in 1978 the hostility between

AMAL and the PRM was beginning to show but, by 1981, there was a complete breakdown. There were several reasons for this. The first was Israel's calculated policy of raising the cost of the presence of the PRM to the inhabitants of the south, by attacking Lebanese villages as well as Palestinian camps. Secondly, the PRM fighters themselves behaved abominably, with accusations of theft, rape, extortion rackets and oppression. It was particularly sad because the PRCS provided health services to all the inhabitants of the south. AMAL played a very significant part in the subsequent history of the Palestinians in Lebanon.

By February 1982 Ariel Sharon, Israel's Defence Minister, had completed plans for a major invasion of Lebanon with the aims of dealing the PLO a knockout blow, forcing the Syrians out and establishing a friendly Christian-led government. It was hoped that this would force the PLO leadership into a 'gilded cage' in Damascus where it would have no independence nor control over the Palestinians in the Occupied Territories.

All Sharon needed was an excuse, and he got it, with the attempted assassination of the Israeli Ambassador in London. The Israeli army was well-armed with US weaponry. The PLO only had the weapons of guerillas, not of an army, so could never be a threat to the Israel Defence Force. They were forced to site the command headquarters, train fighters and store arms in or near the camps, because these were the only areas in Lebanon under their independent control.

Sharon told the Israeli cabinet that he needed only twenty-four hours to accomplish his goals, that he would advance only twenty-five kilometres into Lebanon and the PLO would be smashed. However, the actual timetable of the war turned out to be rather different. Between 6 to 9 June the IDF overran south Lebanon, from 10 to 13 June Beirut was encircled and by 26 June they had gained control of the hills overlooking Beirut. From 27 June to 12 August Beirut was under siege, and then between 21 to 30 August the PLO left Lebanon, only to be followed on 16 and 17 September by the massacres in the camps of Sabra and Shatila.

The war, which was supposed to be a swift, clean, surgical operation, all over in a maximum of seventy-two hours, became a clumsy, bloody campaign which lasted for sixty-seven days. The IDF failed to sweep into Beirut, due to the tenacity of the PLO and

Lebanese fighters. The IDF destroyed the camps, even when all the fighters had been killed or escaped, since Israel saw the camps as the physical, organised presence of the Palestinian people. As one commentator put it, 'The object of the battle is an Israeli attempt to kill an idea, the idea of Palestinian nationality — even when, on August 12, Philip Habib was on the verge of getting a settlement, Beirut was subjected to its most intense bombardment — a compromise without full humiliation of the PLO would risk survival of an idea.'[3]

Sharon had deceived the cabinet about his plan to advance as far as Beirut and only the Prime Minister, Mr Begin, supported him wholeheartedly. Many dissident and questioning voices were heard in the cabinet but Sharon, with the backing of Begin, continued to push north to lay siege to Beirut and the stunned silence from the US government was interpreted as consent. The bombing of Beirut was relentless, even cluster and vacuum bombs were used. Christian East Beirut, the home of the Phalangists, Israel's protegees, even allies, was spared and life continued there normally. Sharon was determined to humiliate the PLO and drive it out, there would be no cease-fire until the PLO agreed to go. This they did. 13,000 left for Tunis on 21 August and Arafat for Greece on 30 August. The multinational force moved in and Bashir Gemayl, the man Israel wanted as President, was sworn in on 23 August. On 10 September the multinational force withdrew, and on the 14 September Gemayl was assassinated. Israel occupied West Beirut on 15 September and on 16 September the Phalangists, under instructions from and cover from the IDF which surrounded the camps of Sabra and Shatila, moved in to liquidate the remaining Palestinian 'terrorists'. 2,000 men, women and children were massacred instead.

Sharon's grand strategy largely failed. It left Lebanon in turmoil, the Syrians in virtual control, and the Palestinians still there — although the Palestinian fighters were exiled they soon regrouped.

Finally the Israelis had risen up in horror. IDF soldiers wondered what they were doing fighting this kind of war and ordinary Israelis cried 'enough is enough'. The IDF tried to brazen out their occupation for three years but they were eventually forced to undertake a phased withdrawal because they were losing too many men. They withdrew, arming everyone before they left, thus fuelling further conflict between the sects. However, they did not withdraw from the Security Zone.

The aftermath of the invasion left the Palestinians in a difficult position. The Lebanese wanted rid of them but no Arab League country would accept them. It had been difficult enough for the US envoy, Philip Habib, to find places of refuge for the expelled fighters. The Lebanese Ministry of Labour refused to issue work permits, but this had little impact as all able-bodied males (9,500 at its peak), were in the huge Israeli prison, Ansar, in the south of Lebanon. The camps had been almost destroyed so many were homeless and for the first year rebuilding was forbidden.

A serious split occurred in the PLO in 1983 — between those loyal to Arafat and 'dissidents', led by Abu Mousa and backed by Syria, based in Damascus. There was a serious confrontation between the two factions in the north, which resulted in the last and final departure of Arafat and the loyalists from Tripoli to Tunis. The majority of those in the camps in the south remained loyal to Arafat but the Beirut camps were divided and the Tripoli ones solidly pro-Syrian. During the camp wars, from 1985-1987, the different Palestinian factions fought amongst themselves but when attacked by AMAL they pulled together against the common enemy. The camps were attacked three years in succession by AMAL forces.

AMAL and the Lebanese villages in the south now began to determinedly resist the IDF. However they no longer supported the Palestinians and tried to drive them out. They did not succeed. In 1988 a decisive intra-Fatah battle, in which the 'dissidents' had Syrian artillery and logistic support, resulted in the fall of Shatila, but all the other camps in Beirut, Tripoli, Tyre and Sidon are still home to 250,000 Palestinians.

1   (Copyright ©1973, 1978, 1984 by International Bible Society. Used by permission of Hodder & Stoughton Ltd. All rights reserved.)
2   David Gilmour, *The Fractured Country* (Sphere Books Ltd, London, 1984, p. 163)
3   Michael Jansen, *The Battle of Beirut* (Zed Press, London, 1982, p. 48)

10

BAPTISM OF FIRE

'Thou wilt keep her in perfect peace
whose mind is stayed on Thee.'

Isaiah 26.3 (New International Version of the Holy Bible)[1]

The third siege of Burj al Barajneh camp in Beirut, from 28 October 1986 until 6 April 1987, by AMAL, the Shi'ite militia, brought home to us in Britain the horrors of the continuing civil war in Lebanon. In 1985 I had retired after thirty years in Nazareth and after handing on my village work to local doctors, had come to live in Edinburgh. Having been told that, in retirement, one does some of the things one never had time to do when working, I embarked on a long-standing dream of studying Arabic and enrolled at Edinburgh University for a degree in Arabic and Islamic Studies. I graduated in 1990 with a second class honours degree and a dissertation on al Razi, a tenth century Persian physician. (He was probably the greatest and most original of all Islamic physicians and wrote the very first treatise on paediatrics.)

As a student I had long vacations, one of which I spent at the University of Sa'ana the capital of North Yemen. It is a beautiful and fascinating country and, as well as studying Arabic, I was able to visit a number of primary health projects and explore the country.

In 1987 I was challenged to apply to work with Medical Aid for Palestinians (MAP), a London-based charity set up in the wake of the Israeli invasion of Lebanon in 1982. The siege of Burj al Barajneh by AMAL had been relieved by Syrian intervention on 6 April 1987 and the situation was relatively quiet. In late June 1987 I therefore found myself in Cyprus with the MAP team, Dr Swee Chai Ang, the Chinese orthopaedic surgeon, Susan Wighton, a Scottish nurse who had survived the siege of Burj al Barajneh, and a group of nurses from Malaysia. Dr Ang was working in Shatila at the time of the massacres and gave evidence at the Israeli Kahan Commission.

We finally got our visas to enter Lebanon and were posted to Burj al Barajneh. It was my first experience of a refugee camp — an UNRWA school, the PRCS Hospital, breeze block houses, some of which had been two or three storeys high before the siege. The camp was really a shambles after the constant shelling, but people were trying to rebuild. Water came from stand pipes and electricity from a crazy network of wires connected to the mains. Only women were allowed to move in and out, so they had to do all the shopping. Burj lies just near the infamous airport highway from which so many Western hostages were snatched. We could see the planes flying overhead and the cars speeding along the highway, yet we were surrounded by AMAL soldiers with their guns trained on us from surrounding high-rise buildings. Haifa Hospital in Burj was quiet when we arrived, so, when the co-ordinator of the Norwegian Aid organisation (NORWAC) under which MAP worked asked me if I would go to a camp in the south, I jumped at the idea. So began my close relationship with Qasmiyeh camp.

Qasmiyeh, about ten miles north of Tyre, is a small 'unregistered' camp which means it was set up after the seventeen official UNRWA camps. It is in two parts, divided by the main road, each inhabited by a different Beduin tribe from the north of Galilee near Safad, al Haib and Hamdoun. It is built on land 'donated' by the local Lebanese landlord, so has no permanency, unlike the official UNRWA camps set up on land leased for ninety-nine years. The people in the unregistered camps are registered with UNRWA, so get the benefits of their medical services, schooling and rations. However the camps themselves get no UNRWA help in repairs and rubbish disposal — these have to be provided by the camp popular committee with money from the PLO. In 1987 there were about 40,000 people living in Qasmiyeh.

The camp is right by the sea but we were prohibited from swimming — Israeli gunboats patrolled up and down. I worked in the PRCS clinic in the camp, some days treating seventy patients including Palestinians, neighbouring Lebanese villagers and even AMAL soldiers from the checkpoints. We were officially an unarmed camp which meant we were supposed to have no fighters with guns. I had a car for my work, because three days a week I travelled north to do a clinic run by the Mousa Sadr Foundation. Mousa Sadr was really the founder of AMAL but disappeared mysteriously. His sister set up the foundation to help the poor Shi'ite

Lebanese in the south who are often poorer than the Palestinians as they get no help from UNRWA.

When there was shooting nearby the young men would rush up to the roof or into the nearby orchards and hide. The only entertainment was to visit the neighbours and drink endless little glasses of sweet tea (no alcohol was allowed inside the camp). Everybody chain-smoked and the men were somewhat addicted to gambling — there was little else to do.

One time I was called in the middle of the night to the house of an elderly man who had died from a heart attack. (One did not go out at night with a light as any movement or light alerted the soldiers and they would start shooting, so I was stumbling about with a tiny torch). The dead man was actually a Lebanese, who had fled because of the shelling in the south, and had taken refuge in the camp. His wife wanted to bury him in his own village but had to apply to the Israelis for permission. She was allowed to go to the burial with only one of her daughters but they were not allowed to stay overnight.

In the house where I lived, I used to wonder why the walls were only half-painted — they looked as though the painter had suddenly thrown down his brush on being called away. I discovered that that is exactly what had happened — AMAL had burst in and dragged him off to their prison and beat him so mercilessly he still carries the scars on his back.

I much preferred the south to Beirut in spite of AMAL. The Syrian army was everywhere in Beirut, the camps were devastated, and the city such a shambles, it was very depressing. My most treasured memory of Beirut is of a visit to a kindergarten run by the General Union of Palestinian Women, in one room of a ruined house in Burj al Barajneh. The children sang for me their patriotic song, 'Baladi, ya baladi' ('My country, oh my country'), and then presented me with a red paper rose which I treasure to this day.

I made many good friends there in Lebanon and therefore followed very closely the unfolding saga of the Palestinians, with the hope that one day I would be able to go back.

11

THE INTIFADA

'Jesus turned and said to them, "Daughters of Jerusalem do not weep for me; weep for yourselves and for your children".'

Luke 22.20 (New International Version of the Holy Bible)[1]

Discerning Israelis, even politicians could see that the conditions under which the Palestinians in the Occupied Territories were living were intolerable. Without the right to vote or be elected, without any control over the government that determined the conditions of their lives, with permission to cross into Israel but without permission to sleep overnight, the Occupied Territories was a powderkeg just waiting to explode. Yet the government was taken by surprise when the Intifada (in Arabic 'the throwing off'), exploded on 9 December 1987, two days after four Palestinians were killed in a road accident involving an Israeli driver.

Ghassan Rubeiz, the Lebanese Middle East Secretary of the World Council of Churches, had visited the 'Holy Land' in December 1986, and was full of foreboding, writing, 'The Palestinians have shown great tenacity in staying on their land, despite the occupier's efforts to take away much of it. By producing more and more rules and procedures to regulate the life of the occupied people, the Israelis have tried to justify their force legally. The Palestinians produce children and the Israelis produce laws. Children need more land, and laws take away much needed land. Two parallel, secret and "civilised" battles are going on inside the Occupied Territories; a battle of permanence and propagation of life faces a battle of a growing legal web to justify force. Explosions of conflict of interest will continue. Where will this situation of rule by force lead? We appeal to the mobilizers of the forces of love and life to lead us into a new era where the Palestinians and the Israelis will recognise each other's needs, history and future.

'The message of the Palestinians in the Intifada to the Israelis is not, "I don't want you". Rather, what the Palestinians wish to communicate to the Israelis is, "I don't want you here, on my land, in the West Bank, in Gaza, in East Jerusalem. I want you as a neighbour, not as an occupier".'[2]

For twenty years, since 1967, the Palestinians in the West Bank and Gaza had lived under a severe military occupation. Immediately after the war of 1967 the Israelis began confiscating land and building settlements. Water also came under the control of Israel's National Water Authority and seventy-five per cent of West Bank water goes now to Israel and the settlements. In the Jordan valley, thirty Israeli settlements use sixty million cubic centimetres of water and only 115 million cubic centimetres is available for 400 Palestinian villages and towns.

Because of land confiscation and water control only twenty-five per cent of the Palestinian population can support themselves by agriculture, which was the traditional way of living. Israel has confiscated one third of the land on the Gaza Strip — one of the most densely populated places on earth — and built settlements for 2,500 Israelis while 600,000 Palestinians live on the rest. Before the Intifada the same problems of lack of agricultural land and water meant that nearly half the Gazan workforce had to cross daily into Israel.

Hospital services in the Occupied Territories also left much to be desired. The nine government-controlled hospitals with 1,001 beds (apart from the one in Ramallah which gets a lot of support from overseas aid agencies) are underfunded, often dirty and with demoralised staff. There are also 853 beds in independent charitable hospitals. This gives a patient/bed ratio of 1.5 beds per 1,000 Palestinians compared with 6.2 beds for 1,000 Israelis. Israel in 1989 spent US$138 on healthcare for each of its citizens but only US$15 for each West Banker. Palestinians have to pay the equivalent of £120 a night unless under three years of age when hospital care is free.

Life for the Palestinians in the Occupied Territories is controlled by hundreds of military orders. Israel controls what may or may not be published, imprisons people without trial, closes universities, schools and newspapers, imposes curfews, demolishes houses and deports suspected leaders of resistance — including some who always called for nonviolent protest, like the pacifist Mubarak Awad who said in the American journal entitled *Sojourners* that, 'It doesn't matter who does the killing — the government, the police, the army, a soldier or a civilian. It is wrong because you are killing a part of God.'

The Intifada moved through several phases. The first phase was a massive protest which took the form of widespread stone throwing. This met a violent response from the IDF which was condemned by the international community. Phase two saw the Palestinians working to consolidate the community-based 'popular' structures, which served both to sustain protest and to create organisational forms independent of the Israeli authorities. Israel's response was an all-out 'war' against these popular structures.

Jehad decided to make a little farm in his garden in Beit Sahour, a largely Christian village near Bethlehem — with chickens and vegetables. It was also practical because of the frequent curfews. Then his neighbours also wanted to do the same, so he started to teach them. This was too much for the occupying authorities, the army moved in and threatened them with arrest — their gardening activities were deemed subversive and must stop.

The authorities imposed a whole range of sanctions against Palestinian agriculture, including sieges at harvest time to prevent crop harvesting or sale, bans on export and uprooting of trees.

The village of Beit Sahour became famous for its campaign to resist taxation in 1989. The people said that they would not finance the bullets to kill their children, the growing number of prisons, the expenses of the occupying army nor the luxuries and weapons supplied to the collaborators. The result was that Israeli tax collectors raided the homes of fifty merchants, took their identity cards stating that the cards would only be returned on payment of the taxes. (A Palestinian can do nothing and go nowhere without an ID card.) They continued to refuse for a year and then troops and tax officials moved in and confiscated goods from businesses and everything from the tax resistants' homes (including all the toys). Then they were arrested. The campaign drew a lot of international publicity and interest and a group of Israeli peaceniks set up a support group.

The following poem was written as the poet watched a man trying to put a roof on his demolished house at Beit Sahour:

'While shepherds watched their flocks by night
a mile away the soldiers dynamite the inn
of the little family whose fifteen year old, like David

threw a stone at the Israeli Goliath but without David's success.
For this crime against the mighty, the lowly are rendered home-
less,
and pitch their tent beside the empty tomb.
The grandeur of the mother
ennobled by suffering;
and the two children standing uncomprehending, and the father
with a jaded resignation
begins again to raise a covering over the foundations.'[3]

Another result of the occupation was the cultivation of a net-work of informers as part of the system of control over the Palestinian population. Individuals and sometimes whole families became part of the intelligence network operated by the Israeli security services. In return for supplying information on local political activists, informers would receive favours from the authorities, including weapons. These informers, or collaborators, also became part of a system of patronage whereby Palestinians in need of some official document from the civil administration, such as a licence to trade or build, were forced to go through the informers, who acted as middlemen with the Israeli-run department in return for a fee.

How to deal with these people became an increasing problem for the Palestinian leadership. At first they were just asked to sever their links and some did so — but, unfortunately, intimidation became more common as the informers became more blatant, and some were killed. Some people who were not informers at all were murdered. The Israeli authorities made a lot of publicity about these 'extrajudicial' killings which did a lot of damage to the 'cause' of the Intifada.

The Intifada entered phase three when the international community began to reformulate its diplomatic stance towards the question of Palestine. The Palestinian National Council, in November 1988, declared an independent state of Palestine, recognised by the majority of the member states of the UN, including the USSR and China but excluding the US and the UK. The PLO leader, Yassir Arafat, recognised Israel's 'right to exist in peace and security', and then the US announced its intention to open a dialogue with the PLO.

In March 1990 the International Fellowship of Reconciliation decided to send a delegation to visit Israel and the Occupied Territories, and I was able to go as the Scottish delegate, almost five years to the day since I had left Nazareth. It had been such a wrench to leave I told myself at the time that I could never go back — to go through the process of leaving a second time would be too traumatic. Now I realised I could not go on working on behalf of the Palestinians if I stayed in Scotland. On this visit we were really able to experience the Intifada first hand and also to meet and talk to people from Israel — 'peace people', Palestinians and government spokespeople who gave us the standard Israeli speech on the need for security.

All the delegates were able to stay in different camps. I stayed in Jabaliya in Gaza, with a family who had one very disabled boy who was ten years old. They live in the standard, two-room breeze block house and the boy was everywhere, restless and almost impossible to control. During the frequent and prolonged house curfews it is forbidden to put even one's nose outside the door, so it was a twenty-four-hour job for his mother to control the boy. There is a local organisation which tries to help and the occupational therapist came to the house, if there was no curfew, just to relieve the mother. This organisation tried to open a day centre for disabled children but the Israelis closed it down, saying it was illegal for people to foregather. My host showed me the title deeds to his father's land near Ashkelon just north of Gaza which were headed 'The Government of Palestine'. He said that he knew he could never get that land back as the port of Ashkelon is built on it, but he would be willing to accept another piece in lieu of it. We went to visit a three-year-old boy who had been standing at the door of the little courtyard which surrounds each house during one of the curfews, when he had been shot in the eye by an Israeli soldier. The army would accept no responsibility, and the family were looking for the money to fit him with an artificial eye. Not surprisingly he was a withdrawn, timid boy.

Dr Hanan Ashrawi — Professor of English Literature at Bir Zeit University in the Occupied Territories and one of the Palestinian negotiators at the Madrid Peace Conference — has written a very moving poem about children like him, as he is by no means the only one.

'From the Diary of an Almost-four-year-old':

Tomorrow, the bandages
Will come off, I wonder
Will I see half an orange,
Half an apple, half my
Mother's face
With my remaining eye?

I did not see the bullet
But felt its pain
Exploding in my head.
His image did not
Disintegrate, the soldier
With a big gun, unsteady
Hands, and a look in
His eyes
I could not understand.

If I can see him so clearly,
With my eyes closed,
It could be that inside our heads
We each have one spare set
of eyes
To make up for the ones we lose.

Next month, on my birthday,
I'll have a brand new glass eye.
Maybe things will look round
And fat in the middle —
I've gazed through all my marbles,
They make the world look strange.

I hear a nine-month-old
Has also lost an eye.
I wonder if my soldier
Shot her too — a soldier
Looking for little girls who
Look him in the eye —

I'm old enough, almost four,
I've seen enough of life,
But she's just a baby
Who didn't know any better.[4]

We came away from our visit profoundly moved by all the suffering we had seen and asked ourselves what we could do.

I personally made three decisions which were to support those Israelis who want to talk with the PLO on the subject of peace; to try and keep the situation on the world's agenda and to help Western Christians to rethink their Biblical understanding of Israel.

The Palestinians and some Israelis were saying that we had given them goods to feed the poor but that they asked also for love — they needed friendship.

In June 1990 the Israel/Palestine Group of Scottish Churches Action for World Development (SCAWD), of which I was a member, hosted a conference in Scotland, which we called 'At the Crossroads of Curse and Benediction: Searching for a Just Peace in Israel/Palestine'. We had among the invited speakers Dr Hanan Ashrawi and Marc Ellis, a Jewish theologian. He called on Jews and Christians to move forward from the Holocaust to a theology of Jewish liberation, in solidarity with the Palestinian people. At the conclusion of the conference, the participants all signed a declaration, calling on Her Majesty's Government to do all in its power to bring about an international conference, under UN auspices, at which the Israeli government and the PLO could negotiate the terms of a peaceful solution.

As the Intifada failed to throw off the yoke of occupation the struggle which had been largely nonviolent became more 'militaristic'. The leaders, many of whom who had been arrested, lost control to the younger men, the *Shibab,* who tried to take the law into their own hands.

The Islamic movement HAMAS (meaning 'zeal' in Arabic), which had formed in 1988 as a branch of the Muslim Brotherhood and had grown from disillusionment with the PLO as the Intifada dragged on, now came to the fore. The Israeli administration had nurtured this movement in the Occupied Territories as an instrument to undermine the PLO with it secular and nationalist constituents. Now they reaped the fruits. HAMAS is working towards an Islamic state and has an uneasy relationship with the PLO. Its militancy and completely uncompromising stance towards Israel has steadily become more popular in the Occupied Territories, even within the Green Line.

1   (Copyright ©1973, 1978, 1984 by International Bible Society. Used by permission of Hodder & Stoughton Ltd. All rights reserved.)
2   Ghassan Rubeiz, *Palestinian Struggle* (WCC, Geneva, 1988, p. 2 pamphlet)
3   Michael Prior, *Christians in the Holy Land* (World of Islam Festival Trust, London, 1994, p. 193)
4   Hanan Ashrawi, *From Intifada to Independence* (The Palestinian Information Office, Netherlands, p. 47)

12

HEBRON

*'So the descendants of Aaron were given Hebron,
a city of refuge.'*

1 *Chronicles* 6.57 (New International Version of the Holy Bible)[1]

Having graduated in July 1990, I was now free to get back to work, medical work. The Intifada was still raging in the Occupied Territories and in August Iraq invaded Kuwait. There seemed little hope of peace and justice for the Palestinians.

In September 1990 I went, at the invitation of MAP on a year's assignment as a kind of consultant paediatrician (one month in every three months) to a small children's hospital in Hebron.

Hebron, which lies about thirty miles south of Jerusalem, in the Occupied Territories, is a very ancient city. Abraham bought the cave of Macphelah there, in order to bury his wife Sarah, and also buried there are Abraham, Isaac and Jacob. King David had his capital there until he captured what became Jerusalem. It is, therefore, a city sacred to Jews, Christians and Muslims. Jews and Arabs are both descended from Abraham, the Jews through Sarah and her son Isaac and the Arabs through Hagar and her son Ishmael — they are, therefore, true blood brothers. I went one day to the Mosque of Abraham, built over the tombs of the Patriachs. Once a Crusader church, it was turned into a mosque after the capture of Hebron by Saladin in 1187. It is now shared by the Muslims of Hebron and the Jews from the new settlements in the area. This particular day the Muezzin was calling the Faithful of Islam to prayer from the minaret and the Jews were streaming into the section of the mosque set aside for their use, under the eyes of the ever present soldiers on guard. Both peoples were going up to worship the same God but were completely ignoring each other. It epitomised for me the deep gulf between these people which has to be bridged.

The Mohammad Ali Hospital For Children in Hebron was built with money given by a 'simple merchant', as he was described to me, from Hebron, who had made a lot of money in Jordan and, instead of building a mosque — which is what most wealthy Muslims do — he built a hospital. The first part was only opened in 1988 with twenty-four cots, including incubators for premature babies, and an outpatient clinic. The second part has still to be completed. The money for the day-to-day running costs of the hospital, is found by the Hebron Red Crescent Society, a local charitable society. The hospital fulfils a real need, as the only alternative is the government hospital, understaffed, underfunded, poorly equipped and expensive for patients. The Mohammad Ali has graded fees according to the ability to pay and no child is turned away so long as there is room.

In October 1990 we were shocked by the massacre at the Haram al Shareef Mosque in Jerusalem (called by the Jews the 'Temple Mount') when the IDF shot dead twenty-one Palestinians. I was in Jerusalem that day and was warned by a friend not to go into the Old City as there had been rumours of trouble as a fanatical group of Jews, the Temple Faithful, were planning to go up to lay the foundation stone of the Third Temple. It was Friday so the mosques were thronged with Muslim worshippers. I went to Ramallah instead, to the Government Hospital, and, while waiting for a lift back to Jerusalem, I realised something had happened — ambulances were arriving and young men were donating blood. There were so many casualties they were being transferred from Jerusalem to Ramallah. I decided that I would only be in the way, being a visitor, so beat a hasty retreat back to Jerusalem. As usual, what actually happened was hotly disputed by the two sides.

As a paediatrician with experience in community and village work my first month in the Mohammad Ali convinced me of the need for some sort of outreach to the children who had been hospitalised. So often they had to be discharged too early because of pressure on beds, or their mothers had to go home to care for the other children or their family had no money to pay. This caused too many readmissions or a very slow improvement at home. I put this need to MAP when I returned to the UK, but then came the Gulf War and the prolonged curfew under which all the Occupied Territories were placed. I could not get back until April 1991.

After the Gulf War, the situation in Hebron had not improved, in fact it had deteriorated. During the curfew the Palestinians had not been able to go to work, nor work in their fields and not even in their gardens, added to which, most of the Palestinians who had been working in Kuwait and the Gulf had to leave. That put a stop to all the remittances on which the people of the Occupied Territories had been surviving, so economically things were very bad.

We were able to start our outreach programme with a young trained health educator and a nurse. There were many hiccups, what with elusive drivers and a very old 'clapped-out' ambulance for home visits (which sometimes caused some consternation when we clattered into a village and the people thought we were bringing home a victim of the Intifada).

We had joy and satisfaction too — Fatmeh, a little girl who at six months weighed only four kilogrammes, became an eight-month beauty with bows in her hair. She went home weighing only 1.8 kg to her family's tent of old sacks fifteen kilometres from the nearest village. Her Beduin family has never been allowed to build a house on their own land as there is an Israeli army camp nearby. Over the years they have become poorer and poorer. They no longer have the traditional Beduin tent of goat's hair, which is cool in the summer and warm and dry in the winter. Fortunately Fatmeh's mother was able to breast-feed her and she thrived. The family had almost nothing — a donkey to carry the water they must walk miles to fetch, and a few hens — yet they insisted on brewing up tea and pressed me to take some of their precious dried yoghourt. They had virtually nothing, yet they gave us traditional Beduin hospitality.

Another little boy, Mohammad, also lived in a tent. His family had a house, four walls and a roof, but they had to use it to raise chickens, to keep them safe and warm because his father had not been able to find any work since the Gulf War. Until the rains came the chickens had to have priority but they did intend to swop round once the chickens had grown.

The mood of the Palestinians, after the Gulf War, was angry and bitter as they saw the double standards the West used — one for Iraq and Kuwait and another for Israel and Palestine. The Palestinians know, as well as anybody else, that Saddam Hussein is a ruthless dictator but they saw him as the one strong leader who seemed to be taking up their cause.

I finished my involvement in the outreach programme in Hebron in February 1992 in the worst winter in living memory.

The municipality would turn off the electricity if the snow was heavy, afraid the ancient electricity poles would come down under the weight of the snow. To keep warm was difficult and to dry anything was just about impossible. It was particularly difficult for the mothers of tiny babies trying to keep them warm, and we had cases of hypothermia in the hospital, a few of whom died, but I am sure we managed to save a few by the teaching we had been able to give the mothers on how to keep them warm.

The families were always most welcoming as we rattled up to their doors — our intrepid driver was prepared to tackle the most daunting looking tracks, even in snow and fog. In their loneliness and isolation they appreciated that somebody cared enough to seek them out at home.

Christina Rossetti's Christmas carol gives a very true picture of what it might have been like that Christmas night so long ago near Bethlehem, only about twenty miles from Hebron:

> 'In the bleak mid-winter
> Frosty wind made moan,
> Earth stood hard as iron,
> Water like a stone;
> Snow had fallen snow on snow,
> In the bleak mid-winter,
> Long ago.'[2]

1 (Copyright ©1973, 1978, 1984 by International Bible Society. Used by permission of Hodder & Stoughton Ltd. All rights reserved.)

2 *In The Bleak Mid-winter* (The Church Hymnary Third Edition, Oxford University Press, 1973, Oxford, number 178)

13

THE GULF WAR

'But let justice roll on like a river,
righteousness like a never-failing stream!'

Amos 5.24 (New International Version of the Holy Bible)[1]

I was in Scotland during the Gulf crisis, praying that the US would not act on its deadline. Surely they knew that Arabs do not work on the principle of deadlines but on the principle of bargaining. However, war was declared and its results were felt well beyond the borders of Iraq and Kuwait. Immediately hostilities started, all the Palestinians in the Occupied Territories were put under a blanket house curfew lasting forty-five days in most of the West Bank, but for 100 days in Daheishi camp, near Bethlehem. The curfew was lifted for two to three hours every three to four days, and in Gaza for only two hours each week. Only women were permitted to leave their homes for shopping and so on. There was no work in Israel for the men and they couldn't work in the fields, so the crops just withered and died.

The West tried to justify what Israel was doing by saying that the PLO supported Saddam Hussein — was it therefore, a surprising response on Israel's part? In actual fact, the day after Iraq's invasion the PLO condemned it. How could they condone the taking of another's land, when they constantly condemned Israel's occupation of theirs? On a practical level, too, Kuwait had been a very important source of funding for the PLO and 350,000 Palestinians were living and working in Kuwait. Remittances from them supported thousands of their relatives in the Occupied Territories. The PLO, therefore, did all it could to bring about a negotiated settlement.

There were some understanding voices. Boaz Evron, an Israeli columnist, wrote, 'With the Intifada going nowhere, the US 'dialogue' with the PLO a waste of time, and the world standing idly by, naturally you grasp at every straw, even if the straw is actually poisoned bait. You become excited at the sight of an Arab leader, who dares to confront all the world and is shaking it from one end to the other, even if you can't imagine living under his rule in your worst nightmare. An Arab state is suddenly treated like a big power, with whom it is not at all easy to deal. This does something to the collective ego. The enthusiasm for Saddam is really the frustration with America, with Europe and with the Israeli left — with all of us who failed to draw back the occupation regime even one inch.'[2]

The West was horrified when the Palestinians cheered as Iraqi scud missiles landed on Israel — was that surprising? When Shulamit Aloni, of the Israeli Citizens' Rights Party, was asked if she was disappointed by the Palestinian response to the Gulf crisis she replied, 'Why should I be disappointed? Have I done anything for them? Has the Israeli Left done anything for them? The Israeli Left are loyal citizens of Israel, supporting the establishment and upholding the security system. Sometimes we think we are different, that we have done something for the Palestinians, we felt we did a lot. *De facto* we did not. The government continues to rule in the Territories — suppressing human rights, destroying, killing and we have a share in it because we have not gone into revolt. We obey the law. We serve in the army ... In short we abide by the rules of the democratic game. And, therefore, we are partners ... all of us. We are a fig leaf for Israeli democracy. The Palestinians have no obligation towards us. We have done nothing for them and they do not owe us anything.'[3]

The Palestinians cheered as the Iraqi scuds fell on Israel. Official figures were of one Israeli killed outright and twelve additional indirect deaths. This compares with Iraqi fatalities of 100,000 to 120,000 soldiers and 5,000 to 15,000 civilians.

A Jewish writer recently asked his mother, a survivor of the Warsaw Ghetto uprising and Maidanek concentration camp, her thoughts during the war as news filtered back that the Russians were bombing German cities. 'I wanted the Germans to die' she remembered, 'I knew I wouldn't live so I wanted them to die too. We cheered the Russians. We wanted them to destroy anything and everything German. We wished them death every second of the day because we faced death every second of the day'. [4]

Former US Secretary of State James Baker had threatened Iraq's deputy Prime Minister Tariq Aziz that the 'allies' would bomb Iraq 'back to the pre-industrial age.'[5] The 'allies' then withdrew from Iraq. The Kuwaiti royal family returned from the safety of their hiding places to reimpose their autocratic rule, and the allies poured in aid. A Lebanese friend, who went to visit her son in Kuwait, in 1992, told me that the signs of the war had gone, all had been repaired. In 1994 Baghdad University was accepting students from the Occupied Territories. Raid, one of 'my babies' born in Nazareth was studying there. He reported that there was enough locally-produced food, but because of the sanctions, there were no luxuries — in particular he bemoaned the absence of Coca Cola! More seriously, the infant mortality rate has risen alarmingly because the hospitals are not able to provide a good service and there is a severe shortage of medicines.

The Palestinians suffered in many ways for their support of Saddam Hussein. Most of those in Kuwait lost their jobs and were expelled. Kuwait had never granted any Palestinian Kuwaiti citizenship even to those born in Kuwait. Some were able to settle in Jordan, a few found sanctuary in the West and others returned to their families in the Occupied Territories and Lebanon.

Their perceived support of Saddam Hussein cost the PLO dearly as it lost the support of its main financial backers, Kuwait and the Gulf states. The PLO has, therefore, found it increasingly difficult to run its organisations, its medical branch, the PRCS, with its clinics, hospitals, schools and kindergartens and to pay the stipends of its martyrs and fighters and their families.

The repercussions of the Gulf War continue to reverberate throughout the Middle East and beyond.

It did, however, move the US to set up what was euphemistically called the Madrid Peace Conference in October 1991, from which a groaning, creaking 'peace process' has been stumbling and limping along. With the end of the Cold War in 1989 the US was left as the only superpower and was determined to press for a solution to the Israel/Palestine dispute. The Madrid conference of October 1991 was the start, not of a UN-sponsored peace conference, which is what the Palestinians wanted, but of a US-brokered process. The US managed to sideline the UN and agreed that Israel should choose the Palestinian representatives and also insisted that the PLO could not be a formal participant. In the event the Palestinian negotiators, Doctors Haidar Abd al Shafi and Hanan Ashrawi demonstrated to the world the reasonableness of Palestinian demands. Alas, however, the US refused PLO officials access to Washington to advise their formal delegates from 'behind the scenes', which had been possible in Madrid, for the negotiating sessions which continued in Washington. The US election of 1992 brought President Clinton to power. During his election campaign he had declared, 'America and Israel share a specific bond. Like America Israel is a strong democracy, a symbol of freedom, an oasis of liberty, a home to the oppressed and persecuted ... If I ever let Israel down, God would never forgive me.'[6] In its increasingly serious financial position and falling popularity the PLO in desperation has conceded to every Israeli demand much to the horror of the Palestinians who do not want to sell their birthright for a mess of pottage.

While the eleventh fruitless round of talks was taking place in August 1993 it was suddenly announced that secret direct talks between Israel and the PLO had been taking place in Oslo under the aegis of the Norwegian government. These had resulted in a decision for formal recognition between the PLO and Israel as a prelude to an open-ended autonomy arrangement starting with limited self-government for Jericho and Gaza. The Oslo Agreement was formally signed by Prime Minister Rabin of Israel and Chairman Arafat on 13 September 1993. The Oslo Agreement consists of a series of principles, of which the first article agrees to the establishment of an interim Palestinian National Authority (PNA), pending an elected council for Palestinians in the West Bank and Gaza Strip. This is for a transitional period not exceeding five years, leading to a permanent settlement based on UN Resolution 242. There are thirteen articles in all but the wording is so vague they allow for a variety of interpretations and it is now obvious that they are grossly flawed. Raja Shehadeh, a Palestinian human rights lawyer in the Occupied Territories, has pointed out that, 'Despite Israel's well-known and Talmudic approach to negotiations the Palestinian team in Oslo did not consult with any legal adviser. No Palestinian jurist was ever present or consulted throughout the process.'[7]

The Jericho/Gaza withdrawal agreement was eventually signed in Cairo on 4 May 1994 but both areas remain tightly controlled by the Israeli army to this day. The agreement of course only applies to the Palestinians living in the Occupied Territories — the Palestinians in the diaspora are consigned to oblivion. Chairman Arafat has got himself into an impossible situation. He is expected to police the increasingly frustrated population of Gaza which is under frequent curfew with its workforce prevented from crossing into Israel to find work. Meanwhile they have to watch helplessly while more and more Arab land is confiscated by the Israelis — in 1995 estimated as being sixty-seven per cent.

Afif Safieh, the PLO representative in the UK, said that he had heard Mr Shamir (at that time the Prime Minister of Israel) say on television, in Madrid, that Israel had a hunger for peace. Afif Safieh's response was, 'We, the Palestinians can solemnly and publicly say we can satisfy Israel's hunger for peace, if ever Mr Shamir abandons his appetite for territory.'[8]

1 (Copyright ©1973, 1978, 1984 by International Bible Society. Used by permission of Hodder & Stoughton Ltd. All rights reserved.)
2 Norman Finkelstein, *Journal of Palestinian Studies* (University of California Press, California, Spring 1992, Vol. XXI no 3, page 65)
3 Finkelstein, *Journal of Palestinian Studies*, p. 60
4 Finkelstein, *Journal of Palestinian Studies*, p. 68
5 Albrecht Metzger, *Middle East International* (Middle East International Publishers Ltd, London, 21 July 1995, page 18)
6 David McDowall, *The Palestinians* (Minority Rights Publications, London, 1994, p.114)
7 McDowall, *The Palestinians*, p. 122
8 Afif Safieh, *A Palestinian Perspective on the Peace Process* (The Center of Policy Analysis on Palestine, Washington, 1991, pamphlet p. 9)

14

RETURN TO LEBANON

'And all work is empty save when there is love;
And when you work with love you bind yourself to yourself,
And to one another and to God.
And what is it to work with love?
It is to weave the cloth with threads drawn from your heart,
even as if your beloved were to wear that cloth.'

Khalil Jubran[1]

At last the way for me to return to Lebanon opened up. MAP saw that the unregistered camps in south Lebanon lacked regular and easily available medical care. They therefore applied for a grant from the UK Overseas Development Administration (ODA) to fund a 'mobile clinic' and I was appointed as medical officer for the project. I arrived in Lebanon in June 1992 and was delighted to find that I would be based in Qasmiyeh camp where I had been in 1987 — it was like coming home.

After I left Lebanon in 1987 the situation had continued to deteriorate, with no real central authority and constant skirmishes between the different protagonists. Syria was, and still is, playing a major role. Hizbullah, the Party of God — founded in 1982 by Lebanese Shi'tes because some Shi'ites were dissatisfied with the new secular leadership of AMAL, and supported by Iran, — was becoming more active, not only in south Lebanon against Israel but also in Beirut where it was responsible for the kidnapping of some of the Western hostages.

Eventually, in October 1989, a pact of national reconciliation was signed by Lebanese Parliamentarians under pressure from Saudi Arabia and the Arab League — as a result hostilities gradually ceased. This pact was called the Ta'if Accords.

In 1991 all the militias, except Hizbullah, surrendered their heavy weapons and disappeared from the streets. The Lebanese army was able to reimpose the authority of the Lebanese government in Tyre and Sidon, removing the PLO fighters from their bases. The civil war was finished at last.

The Palestinians had hoped that their fighters might be re-organized under Lebanese army command as they wanted some defence against Israeli attacks. However, this was not agreed to because the Lebanese did not want to incur any of the results of the Israeli attacks, and Syria, which was a very powerful force in Lebanon, did not want to preserve any strong Palestinian military presence. There was something else too — something more ominous for the Palestinians. Since the outbreak of the Intifada in the Occupied Territories in December 1987, Chairman Arafat seemed to be losing interest in the Palestinians in Lebanon. Arafat's apparent desertion, and then his betrayal of his people in Lebanon reminds me of the Highland Clearances of the eighteenth and nineteenth centuries. John Prebble writes, 'Once the chiefs lost their powers after the defeat of the battle of Culloden in 1745, many of them lost also any parental interest in their clansmen. During the next 100 years they continued the work of Cumberland's battalions. So that they might lease their glens and braes to sheep farmers from the Lowlands and England, they cleared the crofts of men, women and children, using police and soldiers where necessary.'[2]

As a disliked, unwanted, marginalized community in Lebanon the Palestinians have a tough time. My diary, of the two years I shared with them, describes the ups and downs, the joys and sorrows, the hope and the despair and the overriding fear of the future.

6 July 1992

Since arriving in Lebanon in June I have been busy organising clinics for the unregistered camps here in the south, around Tyre. We are going to have two, to serve four camps, both about ten miles to the north of Qasmiyeh and I will work two days in each and the remaining two days (we have Sundays free) I will work in Qasmiyeh. My plans are slowly taking shape but it has meant finding rooms from which to work, as I decided it was better if I was mobile rather than working in the clinic. We have employed two nurses and bought the equipment .

The other day we went to collect the stuff we had ordered from the medical supplier in Tyre. He had assured me that it would all be ready and waiting, but what he meant was he hoped they would all be ready — the order had not been delivered from Beirut — a promise here is often a pious hope!

The Palestinian camps are really little villages, with cement block houses, most of which have a small garden and a vine. The people all originated from the north of Galilee, some are Beduin and some are *fellahin* (farmers). These Palestinian villages are always very clearly designated camps which symbolize the status of the Palestinians here in Lebanon — marginalized, in no way a part of Lebanese society, most definitely not Lebanese citizens. Some of the Lebanese are only too ready to blame the Palestinians for all Lebanon's problems. Since I was in Qasmiyeh in 1987 many people have emigrated, most went to West Germany, either legally, if they have close relatives already there, or illegally, smuggling themselves across the border, but now, Germany like the rest of Europe, has closed the door. Inevitably those with the most initiative have gone, leaving the old, the women, children, the disabled as well as a few who have relatively well-paid jobs with UNRWA and a few who work for the PRCS. Almost the only other work available is seasonal, badly paid, day labour in the nearby orchards owned by wealthy Lebanese. The government prohibits Palestinians from starting their own businesses and they cannot even own a shop, except inside the camps. The government issues about 100 work permits a year for the 250,000 Palestinians! Life for the Palestinians, therefore, lacks purpose and the future looks equally hopeless.

The Lebanese, after their sixteen years of civil war, have also been traumatised but they at least have a country even though part of the south is occupied by Israel, and Syria is virtually in control elsewhere. Some of us from the MAP team went for a picnic on the Litani River just north of Qasmiyeh yesterday with Lebanese friends. Their whole village seemed to be there, enjoying the fast-flowing river and its many pools. The adults swim in their clothes. The women, being Shi'ites, even wear their headscarves but that did not spoil their enjoyment of the water. The conversation came around to the forthcoming elections. One hopes for a nonsectarian vote but religion is still the most powerful force. The Lebanese can enjoy themselves and take an interest in the future of their country, something which is denied to the Palestinians.

2 August 1992

Tonight I am sitting with a mosquito coil burning at my feet. It is still very hot and humid. We had our six-hour ration of electricity this morning so there is none now to drive the fan and the best thing is to sit very still. We have a battery which operates a light in each room, which is a great blessing.

This week our two new clinics are 'in action'. It has taken a lot of pressure and encouragement to get them operating, partly because for both we have had to complete unfinished buildings, paying rent in advance, for the owners to be able to make them habitable. One is under the local mosque (no problem here, as there would be in Saudi Arabia, of having Christians working in such a holy place). Each clinic has two rooms, with toilet, and they are really quite nice and very conveniently situated, within reach of all our clientele. The first day we had twenty patients — maybe some of them came out of curiosity! Already I have seen so much need. I visited an old bed-ridden woman suffering from a stroke. Her son, a schoolmaster, dresses her bedsores, feeds and turns her to the best of his ability.

There are so few eligible men among the Palestinians here, so many have been killed and so many have emigrated, it is becoming a matter of serious concern. One girl, an orphan, lived with her married brother who kept her under his strict control. She heard of a young man in prison who was looking for a wife, so she agreed to marry him. He was allowed out of prison for the wedding ceremony on condition that his brother went into prison in his place. The couple were duly married, the husband went straight back to prison to complete his sentence, but she is now a married woman and therefore no longer beholden to her brother.

Once a week I take 'second-on-call' at the small PRCS Hospital in a camp in Tyre called Burj al Shamali. It is about as well equipped as the Nazareth Hospital was when I started work there in 1955, but it serves a real need.

It would be easy to become disheartened, but there are a few weddings, new babies, ice cream and good telephone links from telephone shops to the UK, even though one has to pay for incoming calls also! I even get free parking in the Tyre municipal car park, as I drive in with vivid red crescents painted on my car.

28 August 1992

I had two breakfasts this Sunday. The first, at 8 am, was with my neighbour, sitting on the stones behind the house, beside the oven on which she had been baking bread since 6 am.

My second breakfast was a couple of hours later, in Tyre, at the home of the Lebanese medical equipment dealer — we ate fresh rolls, olives and cheese and drank instant coffee with milk. I had lambasted him for what I considered his broken promise over the delivery of the stuff for the new clinics but we became good friends! He has not had an easy life as his business was completely destroyed during the Israeli invasion of 1982. He had to build it up again from scratch, but now he has a thriving business and a beautiful home with two bathrooms, glass chandeliers tipped with gold, a colour tv and his own generator. His home is on the ninth floor and the lift only works if there is electricity — six hours some time during the twenty-four hours. He can send his daughters to a private Christian school — they are Muslims, but the Christian schools are the best in Lebanon.

The first general elections in Lebanon for twenty years began on Sunday and they will continue for the next two Sundays. The Maronites in East Beirut are threatening a boycott. They want the election postponed until after Syria's scheduled withdrawal next month — but the Syrians are not going to move so long as the Israelis stay in the south (both are still there in 1995). By the new election law, if one third of the electorate abstains, the results are still valid, but the Maronites claim that such a government would not be recognised, particularly by France.

This has been a month of consolidating the work in the new clinics. I treat twenty to twenty-five patients a day which gives me time to visit the homes. The difficulty of caring for patients with our limited facilities has been highlighted by the case of Nur (meaning 'light' in Arabic), a premature baby who became severely jaundiced. The recognised treatment of placing the baby under a fluorescent light is denied us here because of the intermittent electricity, so we had to fall back on the use of sunlight, which is not considered good for babies by Arab mothers. Fortunately the baby's mother is one of our nurses, so she is sensible and was prepared to try the sun, as well as the folk remedies suggested by all her husband's family, which included a necklace of garlic corms placed around the baby's neck. The baby did very well I am happy to say.

6 October 1992

It is the beginning of autumn in Qasmiyeh now. One of the special things about that season here is the smell of smouldering charcoal in the making, as the people prepare their winter fuel. I wonder about the deforestation but it is only the dead wood from the orchards which the women collect and carry home in huge bundles on their heads. The all-pervading smell and smoke may have something to do with the high incidence of asthma among the population here in the south, but they need the charcoal.

We have identified another needy group of economically poor people near us, the Lebanese Shi'ites, many of whom have fled from the so-called Israeli Security Zone and the constant shelling which goes on almost daily there. Their children are without schooling and without immunisations, so we plan to run a mother and child clinic in Qasmiyeh for these Lebanese and, of course, for any other children who care to come along. The policy of the PRCS has always been to treat everyone regardless of religion or race. Our Palestinian children are immunised and educated up to the age of fourteen by UNRWA.

The Palestinians grow tenser and more apprehensive about their future by the day. Wild rumours circulate. One is that the Israeli government has offered to pay every Palestinian compensation to the tune of US$20,000 for the lands they left in 1948 — presumably if they have the land deeds to prove their ownership. Some do have papers but a lot of the people in and round Qasmiyeh were Beduins from the Hula valley and around Safad, not settled farmers. The 'religious' Muslims say that the Koran forbids the selling of ones homeland but, if Chairman Arafat signs on their behalf, then the money could be accepted. US$20,000 might enable them to emigrate to the fabulous West, which is most people's sole burning desire. (This, of course, turned out to be a fanciful false dream.) Another rumour is that the Lebanese government might offer to some of the Palestinians Lebanese citizenship and the rest would be transported to Jordan. The last place Palestinians want to go is to another Arab country where again they would be refugees, unwanted and stateless. It is not surprising that tempers fray easily nor that the different Palestinian factions vie for supremacy and shootings occur.

Most of the people in Qasmiyeh support Fatah, mainstream PLO, but some of the other camps have people of all the factions and the most bizarre thing can happen. The other day a member of Abu Jihad's faction was shot dead. Young men from all the factions (although one of them had been his killer) turned out for his funeral, to pay him honour as a martyr.

The Lebanese elections did produce a government but whether it has any 'teeth', or any will to rebuild the country remains to be seen. Meanwhile rampant inflation continues. Nobody is starving but the struggle to survive is most people's daily preoccupation.

28 October 1992

Here it is now 'winter' — not that it is cold, nor has it yet rained but the sun now sets at 5.30 pm and within minutes it is pitch dark. There is no street lighting and often no electricity, so there is very little light from the houses and one is struck by the completeness of the darkness and grateful for the myriads of stars and the blessing of moonlight. Of course, daylight comes just as instantly and completely and by 6 o'clock in the morning the sun has risen and the sky is blue.

There are a few gleams of light in Lebanon today. The National Pact of 1943 has taken on a new reality with the newly-elected deputies being people who aren't just faceless names. Of course with the approval of the US and Syria, Elias Hrawi, Maronite Christian, remains as President and the new Prime Minister is Rafiq Hariri, a multimillionaire Sunni Muslim, who has already financed a lot of rebuilding in and around his home town of Sidon. The hope is that, as he already has more than enough money he will be incorruptible! The Speaker is Nabih Berri, head of AMAL, the Shi'ite militia which gave the Palestinians hell until 'peace' broke out. His election has, of course, delighted the Shi'ite Lebanese here in the south and was greeted by a round of machine gun-fire from the soldiers at the nearby checkpoints.

All Saints Episcopal Church in Beirut, badly damaged in the fighting, has been restored, and is to be rededicated by Bishop Kafity of the Diocese of Jerusalem, on All Saints Day, 1 November. This will be a joyous occasion for all Christians, and especially for Palestinian Christians, the Episcopal Church being largely Palestinian from 1948. Lebanon did grant Lebanese citizenship to many of the Palestinian Christian refugees. Most of them do not live in camps but are integrated into Lebanese society fairly well, but one senses that they are still very sensitive about their Palestinian origins and try to keep them quiet.

While checking out the level of child immunisation on a visit to a village up in the hills, we came to a large building — originally the headquarters of a Lebanese political party, then an Israeli army base during the 1982 invasion, then a camp for the AMAL militia. Today it is a Lebanese government school for some of the displaced people who have fled from the shelling in the south. The playground now echoes to the noise of laughing, playing children, instead of soldiers.

24 November 1992

The main event for us here in the south this month was the long-awaited opening of the new PRCS Hospital in Rashidia, a large camp just south of Tyre. It was officially declared open at 1 pm and, at 3 pm the first patient was admitted, a four-month-old baby with meningitis. He had been treated in a private Lebanese hospital in Tyre, the costs being covered by UNRWA, but a private hospital will only keep an UNRWA patient for five days. As his condition was still very serious they referred him to the American University Hospital of Beirut, but he was turned away, as there were no UNRWA beds available. He, therefore, remained at home without any treatment for two days, while his anxious mother waited for Rashidia Hospital to open. Needless to say his condition is very bad (in 1994 he showed signs of severe brain damage). His case certainly proves the need for the PRCS hospitals, which treat all patients for very little and, if really necessary completely free.

I am starting to give some talks, with slides, in Qasmiyeh with the backing of the Women's Union. They run a centre in the camp and we have repaired a small MAP generator and borrowed slides from Middle East Christian Council in Sidon. The first subject I tackled was 'backache' which is very common here. Thirty young women, students of hairdressing and dressmaking, turned up to learn how to prevent back strain. I asked one girl to demonstrate. She lifted the heavy load in the manner which I had explained caused backache and then she asked why she and her mother always awoke with sore backs!

The government of Lebanon seems to be trying to 'get its act together'. The new prime minister has announced a number of anti-corruption measures in the various ministries. The Lebanese pound has been fairly stable, at 1,900 to the US dollar, but the banks ran out of money and a special plane had to be flown to the UK, apparently the only place where Lebanese notes can be printed. We have only paper money. Due to the shortage, salaries had to be paid in 250 notes instead of the usual 1,000, which meant literally sackfuls of money or at least suitcases full!

The rain is battering on the windows, along with thunder and lightning — it has been raining on and off all day and driving is hazardous. On my ten-minute drive home from the clinic this morning, I saw at least twelve cars drawn up at the roadside with their bonnets open and one being pushed from the middle of the road by the soldiers from the checkpoint. Rain is always welcome here, but many people have neither cosy nor watertight houses.

1   Khalil Jubran, *The Prophet* (Pan Books, London, 1991, p. 37)
2   John Prebble, *The Highland Clearances* (Penguin Books, London, 1969, introduction
    p. 1)

15

WAR AGAIN

'Say No to Peace,
if what they mean by "Peace"
is the quiet misery of hunger,
the frozen stillness of fear,
the silence of broken spirits,
the unborn hopes of the oppressed.
Tell them that Peace
is the shouting of children at play,
the babble of tongues set free,
the thunder of dancing feet,
and a father's voice singing'.

Brian Wren, *Say "No" to Peace* © 1986 Stainer and Bell Ltd and Hope Publishing for
USA, Canada, Australia and New Zealand. Reproduced by permission.[1]

25 January 1993

I returned to Lebanon after my Christmas break in Scotland
to find Beirut airport now equipped with red luggage trolleys for
the use of passengers, and even some of the potholes in the roads
filled up. The Lebanese pound has remained steady at 1,800 to
the US dollar, and women picking citrus in the orchards now get
9,000 Lebanese pounds for six hours work instead of only 3,000.
The nurses 'held the fort' in my absence and had spring-cleaned
the clinics and, in one of them, even prepared a little garden for
planting in February. I have been quite busy with an increasing
number of patients, so that we have had to buy more chairs for
them to sit on. We are well supplied with medicines at the moment, fortunately, as there are always a lot of coughs and colds in
the winter. I returned to a week of torrential rain and saw the
difficulties facing a mother trying to keep her children warm and
clean when she has nowhere to dry anything — nappies held near
the charcoal stove to dry only get singed and she certainly cannot
afford to buy disposable ones. A week of sunny days has made all
the difference, although it is very cold at night.

Today we went to Sidon for a preview of an AIDS exhibition which we are going to borrow, and show in the different 'camps' in the south next month. The posters have all been made by the students of the public health course at the vocational training centre run by UNRWA for young Palestinians and they show real imagination. One of our Palestinian doctors here in the south died of AIDS last month. He had studied medicine in Cuba and had then worked in Angola. As it was the people's first experience of AIDS there was tremendous fear and, therefore, a great need for education about it.

4 March 1993

Spring is on the way with cyclamen and anemones reminding me of Nazareth. The AIDS exhibition has been a great success, here in our camp and in the other camps in the south. I think nearly everybody in Qasmiyeh visited and our local staff were able to answer many questions. There is so little to do in the camps people really appreciate something a bit out of the ordinary. Alas, gambling is often a means of recreation, although there was a happy ending to one gambling story. A friend of mine here is the mainstay of her large family. She sews and knits to make a little extra, while her husband gambles. He professed to have become very 'religious', but his wife wondered about the money he kept bringing back, as he is lazy and does not work regularly. One night around midnight two shots rang out in the camp. My friend, suspicious as to her husband's whereabouts, took his gun (this is supposed to be an unarmed camp!), loaded it, and crept out of the house. Seeing a light in a nearby uninhabited shed, she peeped through the keyhole. There was her husband, gambling with three of the poorest men in the camp, from whom he was taking the money, so she shot twice in the air. The men were terrified, as much of the Lebanese army at the checkpoint as of her, but she said she would take the full responsibility and tell the soldiers what had happened if they investigated. 'How can you take food from the mouths of the children of these men?,' she accused him, and said if she found him at it again she would shoot at him. She returned the money he had won. She had a mother's heart for the other men's wives and children.

Next month we expect Miranda, a physiotherapist from New Zealand, who has worked for MAP in Hebron, to join our team here in the south. A sister organisation, Malaysian MAP, is going to provide the equipment for us to have a small laboratory in the clinic here in Qasmiyeh as well, so we are improving the services we provide.

2 April 1993

Lebanon changed to summertime on Sunday, but some people refuse to change, which can cause misunderstandings when one arranges an appointment and forgets to confirm on which time the other person is working! However, it means longer light in the evenings and tonight people were sitting on their flat roofs, talking, drinking tea, enjoying the spring air and the view of the sea.

Over the three days holiday of the Ramadan feast I was able to make two interesting visits. The first was to the Evangelical School for the Blind in East Beirut. Camille, a young Christian Palestinian from Tyre has been awarded a scholarship by the Church of Scotland to study 'Mobility for the Blind'. He is very keen to work with the blind and has taught himself Braille. The director of the school welcomed us warmly and is delighted that Camille will be studying 'mobility' in the UK. There is nobody in Lebanon, Syria or Jordan with such a skill, so he will be able to provide a much needed service when he returns.

My second visit was to Byblos (Jbail) on the coast, to the Armenian Orphanage called 'The Birds' Nest', where I sponsor a boy, Edie, through the Bible Lands Society. It was my first visit, as East Beirut is another world from the Palestinian refugee camps in the south. The orphanage, now staffed by three Armenian Orthodox nuns and a lay staff of Armenians, was started by a Danish woman in 1915 for 100 orphans from the Turkish massacres. There are now 138 children in the school, and it is a beautiful place, with a magnificent new kitchen of superb workmanship. Edie is a solemn little eight year old, said to be a good student but his English and Arabic being limited, and my Armenian nonexistent, communication was limited.

We later visited the 'antiquities' in Byblos, which include a Crusader castle and a Roman amphitheatre. We were actually charged for admission, and there were some other tourists, even some Japanese complete with cameras, so Lebanon is slowly returning to normal!

1 July 1993

Qasmiyeh and the other camps are full of summer visitors from Europe, back to spend the summer with their families. Those who emigrated ten or more years ago have done well, and some of their children have found work in government jobs or banks. If both parents are Palestinian the children will speak Arabic, but if the mother is European, the children, sadly, will not speak Arabic. The family tie is still very strong but one fears that it may be lost by the next generation.

Miranda, who has become my flatmate, has developed a good outreach programme here in the camps, especially for the children with special needs, and for some of the elderly. UNRWA, which provides schooling for all Palestinian children up to the age of fifteen, is going to try and integrate some of the children with special needs into their schools, but they have such large classes it is not going to be easy. In the past these children have just been left to rot at home, so it is a move in the right direction. 'Save the Children Fund' is also going to try to admit the smaller ones with special needs to their kindergartens.

I decided we should do follow-up visits on the babies we had seen at birth, and it has been a joy to find how healthy and well cared for most of them are at three and six months and still breast fed. A little quiz of the mothers, as to how they would cope if their baby had an attack of diarrhoea, revealed that they are well informed.

6 August 1993

The war has rather overshadowed events this month — Israel suddenly started a bombardment of the whole of south Lebanon. Life is now slowly returning to normal, the workmen are putting the finishing touches to the new clinic next door and we are just back from enjoying a cold drink at a cafe on the nearby Litani River. People who fled from the bombardment are returning home and, this weekend, we hope to visit the exiles in Marj al Zahour and find out how they fared during the war.

This war was unlike any other I have experienced — a ferocious air and sea bombardment of a defenceless people. Lebanon has no airforce and an army made up of the disbanded militias. Israel knew exactly the targets they wanted — the bases of the radical Palestinian groups and the Hizbullah strongholds. They could have come in with land forces and probably destroyed them more effectively, but that would have cost Israeli soldiers' lives which Israel could not accept, so they chose an aerial and naval bombardment instead. The women here will tell you that they could cope with Israeli soldiers, because during the invasion of 1982 they behaved decently towards them. A young woman in Qasmiyeh asked her mother-in-law when we were talking about the flight of the Palestinians in 1948, 'But why did you flee? You knew the Israelis would not have harmed you'. She was comparing them with AMAL from her youthful experience in the 1980s, but her mother-in-law just said, 'We were frightened'.

People in Lebanon are terrified of air attacks. Memories of the bombing of Beirut in 1982 are still so vivid, and the people fled. Each day the names of villages which would be attacked were broadcast and the people just upped and fled north, even though they had nowhere to go, except the streets of Beirut. It was the same infectious panic which had caused the Palestinians to flee in 1948. I had wondered if the Lebanese might have stayed for fear that their land would be taken by the Israelis — there are some with expansionist aims to take over south Lebanon — but the fear of aerial bombardment was greater. My only fear is of being buried under a falling building, so I chose to stay in my house, knowing that Qasmiyeh would not be directly targeted, as it is an unarmed camp, pro-PLO, and the PLO is part of the peace process. The aim of Israel was to force the Lebanese villagers to petition their government to control Hizbullah. The bombardment did result in the Lebanese army being deployed in the south and some villages, which had suffered badly, asked for the Lebanese army to come in instead of Hizbullah. Hizbullah, supported by Iran, wasted no time in getting supplies into the bombed villages to help in repair of the houses. The greatest anger is, however, against Israel, which still occupies the security zone in which Israel's surrogate Lebanese army operates.

During the war I heard a spine-chilling rabbi talking on Kol Israel English language news broadcast on the radio. He said that Hizbullah, Islamic Jehad and even the PLO are evil and, therefore, it is Israel's divine right and duty to destroy them, because God said in the Old Testament, that the Jews must not have any dealings with evil. They cannot then negotiate with evil, and on and on he went. The enemy is no longer a human being but a personification of evil. Hizbullah also believe that it is their Islamic duty, written in the Koran and therefore decreed by God, to destroy the Jews. With such opposing enemies there seems little hope of reconciliation, humanly speaking, but, thank God for the New Testament, with its ministry of reconciliation. People have had enough of war and killings — this one has really shaken them.

1 *Praising A Mystery,* Hope Publishing Co (1986). Distributed in Europe by Stainer & Bell Ltd.

16

PEACE AT LAST?

'When a man's ways are pleasing to the Lord, He maketh even his enemies to live at peace with him.'

Proverbs 26.3 (New International Version of the Holy Bible)[1]

10 September 1993

This month has witnessed momentous developments in the Middle East with the signing of an accord between the PLO and Israel for Palestinian autonomy in the Gaza Strip and Jericho. How the two will be connected has not been explained, although there is talk of a new 250-kilometre road being built — bypassing Jerusalem, of course! The Palestinians here are very angry and in the deepest despair; all these years of exile, war and suffering would appear to have been in vain. They feel they have been betrayed by Chairman Arafat. In an interview on Lebanese radio the Leader of the PLO in Lebanon said to Arafat, 'You seem to have forgotten the three million Palestinians outside the Occupied Territories', to which he replied, 'In Lebanon, they are a fact of life', implying that they are no longer the responsibility of the PLO. The Prime Minister of Lebanon has said that Lebanon will never, ever give the Palestinians residence status. Arafat has successfully forfeited all the support he once had here, as the Palestinians naturally wonder what is going to be their future. Mr Rabin, also, has his own serious problems in Israel. The Israelis are deeply divided. An Israeli settler, interviewed on the radio, damned his government in the most vicious terms. If they are not prepared to give up such a minute and unimportant part of the 'Land' they are obviously not interested in peace.

The good news is that we have moved up into our new clinic in Qasmiyeh, which is bright and airy and pleasant for work. Last Sunday I went with Camille — our prospective Church of Scotland bursar — and his parents to his grandmother's house in the Shouf mountains. It happened to be 'Orthodox Movement' Sunday, so there was a special service in the Greek Orthodox Church, attended by Bishop Khudr, Bishop of Mount Lebanon. In the 1940s there was a revival in the Orthodox Church in Lebanon in which George Khudr played a very vital part and he helped to set up the Orthodox Youth Movement, so, now in his eighties, it was fitting that he should be celebrating with the youth of today. It is still a lively church with many young people attending. After the three-hour service there was lunch for everybody, and then Arabic music and dancing. I always appreciate hearing church bells instead of just the five daily 'calls to prayer', shouted from the mosque in Qasmiyeh.

We have another young Palestinian student setting off for Scotland. Najah, from Shatila camp in Beirut, has been awarded a bursary, given by the students of Glasgow University, to study nursing management.

10 October 1993

Little did I think that I would ever see the Prime Minister of Israel shaking hands with the Leader of the PLO. It was a tremendous breakthrough, and, for some, a sign of hope, but, as I watched the ceremony on TV in my neighbour's house here in Qasmiyeh, their stony silence as they saw the last nail being hammered into the coffin of their hopes and dreams of returning to their homeland, meant that I had to keep my feelings to myself.

The sense of betrayal the Palestinians feel here is very deep. When he recognised the state of Israel, Chairman Arafat relinquished all claim to those parts of Palestine which are the present state of Israel, including Haifa, Acre and Galilee from which the Palestinians living in Lebanon originally came. The Palestinians of the Occupied Territories can now look forward to eventually having their own Palestinian state, but Israel has made it clear that the people who left in 1948 will not be allowed to return, neither to Israel nor to the new entity Gaza/Jericho First.

In the 1920s a wealthy Lebanese, a one-time Prime Minister of Lebanon, owned vast tracts of land in Lebanon and Palestine. He practised what was really a feudal system, Palestinian peasants lived on his land and worked it for him and he registered them as Lebanese citizens. Later he sold his land in the Hula valley to the Jewish Agency and in 1948 these peasants fled to Lebanon. Today, those who can prove their descent from those who fled from that area in Mandated Palestine, have once again been given the option of applying for Lebanese citizenship. Many people from Qasmiyeh and the nearby camps have done so. It has meant countless visits to various offices to collect the right papers and the exchange of a good deal of money, but, by the end of September when the offer closed, thousands had applied and now wait to see what will happen. Some, as a matter of principle, refused, saying that they are and will remain Palestinian.

Lebanon is famous for its cedars — a cedar tree figures on the national flag and the army insignia — so a trip to the cedars is a 'must'. We MAP volunteers went to see them a few weeks ago and at first I was disappointed — all I could see were completely bare mountains, towering above us. They are, of course, covered in snow in the winter, so above the snow line there cannot be any trees and when one looks closely at the apparently barren brown soil one sees that it is carpeted in a wonderful variety of Alpine plants which can live and grow under the snow and then flower in the summer. When we enquired if there was any snow left, the Syrian soldiers at the checkpoint said there was none. Then they beckoned us to look down into a valley where the shepherds had gathered snow into huge balls, covering them with blankets to preserve the snow, which they use for watering their sheep in the dry season. The Beduin always know how to adapt to adverse conditions.

There is only one small forest of cedars left — they have been damaged by storms and war, used for firewood and hideous souvenirs — and now the Society for the Cedars of Lebanon is working hard to preserve the remaining trees, some of which are hundreds of years old. They have built a boundary fence, charge an entrance fee, laid out paths and even placed rubbish bins! The cedars are one of Lebanon's most priceless treasures, so it is good that they are now being cared for by the Lebanese themselves.

10 December 1993

1 December was International AIDS Day so, on 2 December, we went to the UNRWA school here, in Qasmiyeh to give a presentation on AIDS. It was for the first time a combined effort between MAP and UNRWA, with the UNRWA doctor giving a talk and then Rehab, who works with me, showing slides. We did three sessions to three different classes and it went very well with the students asking questions.

Lebanon moves slowly towards normality. The museum in Beirut has been reopened — it suffered badly in the war as it was on the Green Line between East and West Beirut — the 'museum crossing' became famous as the main crossing point for the divided city. The curator is afraid to display any actual exhibits — they had been walled up behind concrete to preserve them — so there are just photographs of things at the moment.

1 February 1994

Occupation by one country of another is always an ugly thing and brings out the worst in the occupying power. Syria is, to all intents and purposes occupying Lebanon. The Lebanese government has to defer to Damascus for every important decision.

Everybody was, of course, saddened by the death of Basil Assad, President Assad's eldest son and heir-apparent in a motor accident, but Lebanon has had to show publicly that it is in mourning with the closure of shops and long prayers in the mosques. I was privileged to be visiting a Syrian Christian pastor and his wife in Beirut, the night of the funeral, and they shared with me their belief that the young man's death is a real tragedy for Syria. On the death of such a powerful leader as President Assad, if there is no one to fill the vacuum there could well be a power struggle and more bloodshed.

A young Palestinian bride had to come from her home in Beirut for her wedding in Qasmiyeh on Saturday, the day of Basil Assad's funeral. Her family felt it wiser to tell the Syrian soldiers at the checkpoint, just beside their house in Beirut, that they were taking their daughter to be married. The soldiers said that they could go but, if they heard one note of music or rejoicing they would come and blow up the whole house. Arabic hyperbole maybe, but the Syrians are so feared the family took the threat seriously and crept out of the house. Here in the south the Syrian presence is not so evident so they were able to have a joyful wedding once the bride arrived in Qasmiyeh. There are, of course, good Syrians, as there are good Israelis, but what the people who live under the occupation see is the brutality.

Last week we were able to start work in our new laboratory in Qasmiyeh. We have, of course, had a few teething problems connected with generators, stabilizers and transformers because of our erratic electricity supply. I am sure, however, it will soon be a useful service for the surrounding population, saving them expensive trips to town.

This Sunday I was able to join a small Protestant congregation for worship in Sidon. They are now meeting monthly in the Evangelical school there. The school has a student body of 3,000, only sixty-five of whom are Christian, so it is a real witness in Sidon. Their church was badly damaged in the war but they have got money to repair it. The Christians here in the south of Lebanon, although a minority, are respected by the Muslims, especially if they do not compromise their Christian faith — if you are a Christian then be seen to be a Christian.

25 February 1994

This is the month of Ramadan, the thirty days of fasting from sunrise to sunset, when a Muslim really identifies himself or herself as a Muslim, as it is very obvious who is and who is not fasting. Although the men are lethargic and short tempered (more for want of a cigarette) the women are as busy as ever preparing the food for the breaking of the fast. The meal must be ready exactly as the sun disappears over the horizon, easily seen from Qasmiyeh as it dips below the Mediterranean, and then we wait for the call from the mosque. One sees people hurrying from house to house with dishes of food for friends and neighbours, for nobody must go without, for it is Ramadan Kareem, best translated, I think, as generous. There is a favourite Ramadan prayer, 'For I have done my duty in hospitality to every guest, I am Thy guest, let my guest portion this night be Paradise'. There is a feeling of camaraderie — the whole fast is made null and void by any argument — so disputations have to be postponed. In the south, Hizbullah can continue firing rockets into Israel, as they see their war against Israel as 'holy war' and, therefore, legitimate even in Ramadan.

During Ramadan, all day and every day, on something like thirty-six channels, there are special TV programmes and most certainly not all religious ones! Some are Lebanese comedy shows. The Lebanese government are more generous with the electricity during Ramadan, and we often have it all evening and all night.

The extent of the *Hijra* (the emigration) from Qasmiyeh to Germany was brought home to me very vividly the other day, when I was watching the video of the wedding of a young man from here who left recently to marry a relative whose family have been in Germany for some years. The wedding party, the music, the dancing, the dress could have been anywhere here and I found that I recognised in the video as many friends there as I have here. Nearly everyone here has someone in Germany and they could not survive without their remittances.

The nurses to whom I am teaching paediatrics are a noisy lot, twenty-three young men and women who are much less disciplined than our nursing students in Nazareth! We had to space out the desks for the first test today to stop them cheating! They are also of a much lower academic standard. They are the generation who grew up in the years of the fighting in Lebanon so have had very chequered school careers. I was pleased, therefore, that six of the twenty-three gained really high marks.

We are enjoying the mothers of the children in the 'Save the Children Fund' kindergartens who are attending a series of talks we are giving. They attend regularly and listen and ask questions. Rehab, who works with me, has been translating for me as she said that the mothers were so busy watching me talking Arabic that they did not listen to what I was actually saying! She is getting quite adept as a translator and fields the questions. It will be useful for her as she hopes to start her nurse training after I leave.

We were all deeply shocked by the massacre in the Mosque of Abraham in Hebron on 24 February 1994. A Jewish religious zealot, Dr Baruch Goldstein, entered the mosque and opened fire on the Moslem worshippers marking the end of Ramadan. Twenty-nine were killed before he was overpowered and killed by surviving worshippers. Israeli troops on guard at the mosque failed to intervene, except to shoot dead another six Palestinians. At the funeral of Dr Goldstein, Rabbi Perrin said, 'One million Arabs are not worth a Jewish fingernail.'[2] The hatred between some of the inhabitants of this so-called Holy Land is all prevailing.

27 March 1994

This is Holy Week. While the hillsides are covered in flowers and people are out gathering herbs to cook, eat or to make into the popular herbal medicines, all around us death and destruction continue and hatred is driving people to carry out the most terrible deeds. The Israeli army took over the roof of the Mohammad Ali Children's Hospital in Hebron (where I used to work) for a shoot-out with antitank missiles, against HAMAS supporters. Here in south Lebanon a school bus was shot up during an Israeli incursion into sovereign Lebanese territory and several little girls were killed. In East Beirut, one Sunday recently, a bomb exploded under the altar of a Maronite church killing ten worshippers and injuring many more. At first the blame was laid at the door of Mossad, the Israeli Secret Service, and then at the door of the Muslims, who are said to be angry about the proposed visit of the Pope to Lebanon because the Vatican recently opened diplomatic relations with Israel. However, it has now been discovered that the perpetrators were eight Maronite Christians. So-called Christians killed their innocent fellow Christians in order to make a political statement and destabilise the government. I find it all incomprehensibly horrifying. In the Middle East everybody has to have a religious label — what they actually believe or practice is irrelevant.

The service for the World Day of Prayer which was on 4 March was written by Palestinian women from Jerusalem. I was able to attend the service held in the Near East School of Theology (NEST) in Beirut, and found it very moving. We used the liturgy in English and the following Sunday it was repeated in Arabic in church. The dean of NEST, who took the service and is the chairperson of the local organising committee, told me that she liked the service in English better, perhaps, she admitted, because in Arabic, her mother tongue, the words were much more meaningful to her. Words like imprisonment, torture and homelessness really spoke to her, when she read them in Arabic, of the sufferings of her people.

Vedran Smailovocof from Sarajevo has been playing his music in the streets of Belfast. He believes that what is happening in Sarajevo is not about ethnic strife — and maybe we could add about religious strife — but about exploiting people's fears and differences as a way to gain power and political advantage.

24 April 1994

My time here is drawing to a close so I am delighted that we have found a local organisation which is willing and able to continue the work — it is called Popular Aid for Relief and Development (PARD). It is similar to the Galilee Society for Health, Research and Service (GSHRS) which I helped to set up in the 1970s and which has gone from strength to strength since then. PARD is run by Palestinians and is a recognised charity in Lebanon, helping anybody in need. It is just as interested in environmental issues and health education as in curative medicine so is exactly the kind of organisation for which I have been looking. It has the language, the personnel, the contacts and the sponsors to really get things done. I have noticed that Palestinian women are better than the men in getting things done. The men still have a 'war mentality', they suffer from the well recognised 'disaster syndrome', which makes them say, 'Things are so awful and so hopeless nobody can help us. We have borne the brunt of the struggle and if we are pushed to the wall and everything collapses, so be it.' The women are less fatalistic.

I had two encouraging experiences this month. The first was an Easter Sunday visit with the German-speaking Protestant congregation from Beirut, to two Lebanese Christian villages near Sidon which are being rebuilt. They were destroyed in the fighting in 1985, and so all the people left, but now they are returning and, with the help of the government, the UN Development Fund and the Middle East Christian Council, life is returning to normal.

The second event was in Tyre when my two nurses accompanied me to the Evangelical School there, which has over 1,000 students. We set about vaccinating 130 of the girls against German measles, with much hilarity, shouting and jumping about, in fact we created chaos in the school that day! UNRWA gave the vaccine, which was surplus to their needs (as all our Palestinian children are vaccinated in the UNRWA clinics) so we offered it to this Lebanese school. It was good that the Palestinians were able to share something with the Lebanese, many of whom are just as poor. Some blame the Palestinians for all the woes of Lebanon over the past twenty years.

A final note on the return of normality to Lebanon — I nearly got a parking ticket in Beirut the other day, and actually saw an empty car parked near me being issued with one!

15 July 1994

I left Lebanon at the end of May. After two years of living and working there it was difficult to leave all my friends and colleagues and the MAP volunteers from all over the world — China, England, India, Ireland, Malaysia, New Zealand and Nigeria — and our Lebanese co-ordinator from the Druze community.

One of the best things I did, I believe, was to see the need for a physiotherapist in the south, and the best thing MAP did was to recruit Miranda from New Zealand, with her experience of working in Saudi Arabia, Egypt and the Occupied Territories. She has built up an excellent service for the disabled in the camps. She manages to 'root' them out, and then helps to make their lives easier by, for instance, advising them on adaptations to their houses, (usually financed by UNRWA), helping to get them wheel-chairs or other appliances and taking them on picnics to the sea. MAP is also continuing to fund her project while she trains some local people as rehabilitation assistants.

The quarter of a million Palestinians in the camps are deeply distressed and fearful about their future. They do not know, and, it seems, nobody else knows or at least is saying where they are going to live. Lebanon does not want to give most of them citizenship, nor even work permits, they will never be able to go 'home', to Galilee in Northern Israel, nor will they be allowed by Israel to live in Gaza/Jericho. No country in the world, except Libya, is willing to accept them unless they already have a very close relative long resident in the host country and the promise of a job. That is the situation in which I had to leave my Palestinian friends.

1   (Copyright ©1973, 1978, 1984 by International Bible Society. Used by permission of Hodder & Stoughton Ltd. All rights reserved.)
2   David McDowall, *The Palestinians* (Minority Rights Publications, London, 1994, p. 123)

17

VOICES FROM 'THE MEADOW OF FLOWERS'

'How can we sing the songs of the Lord while in a foreign land?'

Psalms 137.4 (New International Version of the Holy Bible)[1]

'On 17 December 1992, Israel deported 415 Palestinians from the Occupied Territories to south Lebanon for a period of two years. The mass deportation was carried out following the killing that month of six men from Israel's security forces by Palestinians. Following the cabinet's decision to deport a "large number" of Palestinians the authorities were allotted very little time to prepare a list of names. Within a period of hours the security authorities collected hundreds of names, though no evidence — not even after the fact — was adduced against a single one of the deportees. The hundreds of candidates for deportation were rounded up from detention facilities or taken from their homes and placed on buses. They were not informed of their destination, nor were families notified. Despite the blackout imposed by the military censor, several organisations and attorneys heard about the mass deportation in progress, and a number of petitions were submitted to the High Court of Justice that night. After some fourteen hours of deliberation, in the course of which the deportees remained on the buses, blindfolded, hands tied behind their backs with steel bands, the High Court of Justice sanctioned the completion of the deportation. The deportees were thereupon transferred to Zumriyah Pass at the northernmost point of the Israeli "security zone" in south Lebanon. The Lebanese army prevented the deportees from continuing north, and they were left in an area between Lebanese- and Israeli-controlled territory — a "no-man's-land" called Marj al Zahour meaning "meadow of flowers". From then on, the Israeli government maintained that the deportees were in an area controlled by the Lebanese and thus were the responsibility of the Lebanese government, while the latter maintained that Lebanon had not permitted the entrance of the deportees into its territory and so the Israeli government was responsible for them. The Lebanese set up a dirt barrier, while the Israelis blocked off the Zumriyah Pass and mined the road leading to it.'[2]

After a few days the International Red Cross and UNRWA were allowed to bring in tents, food, mattresses, heaters, water and some medicines and a camp was set up. The men themselves would never call it a camp as they did not want to be part of a new Palestinian refugee camp, so they liked to call it a 'station' along the way. Later the Lebanese decided to prohibit Red Cross and UNRWA supplies coming in and Israel also prevented the provision of any kind of aid from their side. This is where MAP volunteers came in, and we made regular visits until the last of the men crossed back on their way home.

In the second half of the twentieth century, Israel is the only democracy which, alongside dictatorships and totalitarian regimes, employs the practice of deportation of residents as a punitive measure. The Fourth Geneva Convention of 1949 prohibits absolutely the deportation of any resident from an occupied territory.

The only people allowed in to visit the exiles were the press — Lebanon wanted as much publicity as possible but did not want any aid to get to the men from the Lebanese side. The only way for us to get in was to get press passes from the Lebanese Ministry of Information in Beirut. Nurse Mary and myself were accredited to a London-based Arab newspaper and every three or four weeks we had to go to get our passes renewed. As a temporary newspaper correspondent I had, of course, to submit my reports which trace the story of the year the exiles spent encamped in Marj al Zahour. They were always insistent that they were exiles, not deportees — one is deported from a country which one has entered illegally but exiled from one's own country, albeit it is occupied.

Throughout their year of exile three of us from the MAP team, Nurse Mary, Dr Yoga and I, visited the men regularly and, as we were affiliated to the press corps, we had to write dispatches describing the Palestinians' lives in exile. These are my reports from the No Man's Land between Israel and Lebanon called Marj al Zahour. These are the 'Voices from a Meadow of Flowers'.

21 January 1993

I have no qualms about calling myself a journalist at the frequent military checkpoints which we have to pass, as I am reporting to the world on what I have seen and heard.

We carried with us gifts of food and medicines, well camouflaged, as we set off on the two-hour drive from Beirut over the mountains. The station is on the rocky hillside, beside the road so can be reached by car. There are forty tents and the men are grouped according to their home villages or towns in the Occupied Territories, according to their own wishes.

The men's lives are highly organised and disciplined by a series of committees, under the leadership of Dr Ghantisi from Gaza. He has emerged as the natural and accepted leader. We have dealt mainly with the medical men, of whom there are ten, but there is also a public relations officer — a nurse who helps in the orientation of all 'visitors' and the press.

They have collected all the medical supplies in one tent and the doctors see around sixty patients a day. They have an adequate supply of essential medicines at the moment, but they dread any exile needing surgery. One man developed a threatened intestinal obstruction and they tried to take him into Lebanon (any approach to the Israeli side is met by fire) but they were refused permission. Fortunately the man made a spontaneous recovery. Now there is a man who slipped on a stone while collecting water and has possibly broken his ankle. He too was refused entry into Lebanon so they are having to manage him with elastic bandages and rest.

They are all devout Muslims, but several we spoke to denied having any connection with HAMAS. They are practically all bearded and because most devout Muslims are bearded, they were probably, to the Israelis, 'marked men'. We found only bewilderment and incomprehension as to why they had been picked up, some from their homes and some from prison where they were being held under administrative detention. Not one of the men had been given even a token trial, and the constant question is, 'What crime have we committed?' It certainly looks as though the 'cream' of the Islamic community in the Occupied Territories has been taken.

Their days are well organised with collecting wood (now getting scarce as they are on a barren hillside) and water. The cleanest drinking water is from the river several kilometres walk away, but there is non-drinkable water a bit nearer. There are so many students among the exiles they have set up their own university since there are plenty of teachers and the students want to write their exam papers.

While we were there the sun was shining and it was dry but snow-covered Mount Hermon is clearly visible so as the sun sets it becomes bitterly cold, and then the exiles retire to their tents for the night. I think the job of just keeping alive takes up so much time and energy there is little left for brooding but they are deeply resentful at the injustice inflicted on them.

30 January 1993

The second last army checkpoint searched the car very thoroughly, even our personal belongings, and kept, until we returned, all my reading material — my Bible and the *Guardian* — not a word of newsprint allowed in to lighten the men's boredom! Our papers were in order and our 'gifts' which were well hidden were not found.

It was good to be going back as we had had such a warm welcome from the men. It was a nice sunny day but the nearest water supply is now reduced to a trickle and the river is also drying up, so the men would really welcome rain and snow to bring them water.

The men are determined to stick together and to return as a group because they were exiled as a group. They do not want to give Israel the chance of putting them on trial one by one, a process which they fear could spin out for decades to come. They asked for money to buy sheep to slaughter which they could get from the Lebanese villagers nearby. This would give them fresh meat (Arabs are great meat eaters) but they ask for very little considering their great need — only to go home and get on with their jobs.

12 February 1993

It was a cold and cloudy day with snow still piled on the sides of the road over the mountains, and Marj al Zahour was a sea of sticky mud, but at least, the men now have plenty of water.

Professor 'Abd al-Fattah al-'Aweisi of Hebron University, a graduate of Exeter University, talked to us in the Ibn Taimih University, held on the hillside in a kind of amphitheatre. There are now eighty-eight students and they have been taking a course in Palestinian studies! Professor al-'Aweisi set the papers for the 'finals' on 14 February 1993 and he will send the results to various universities, through the press. We could see the students walking up and down studying from their notes. They have no books so the teaching has had to be from the minds of the teachers, but Professor al-'Aweisi has already published ten books and his knowledge is impressive. The next course will be in Islamic culture. They have named their university after Ibn Taimih, the famous Islamic thinker, a native of Syria, who was also exiled and imprisoned but who continued his work from wherever he happened to be.

A CNN team spent two days with the exiles, bringing their own tent and supplies with them, which they donated to the men when they departed. The CNN tent which is higher than the others has been made into the clinic and one of the doctors has put up shelves and an examination table. There are five neighbouring Lebanese villages, which used to be served by the Lebanese Red Cross, which is now forbidden to enter the area, so the Palestinian doctors from Marj al Zahour are walking to these villages and treating the people.

I am wondering if Israel has expelled these men not because it really believes they are terrorists but because HAMAS does not agree with Israel's ideas on Palestinian autonomy, a powerless entity which the Palestinian negotiators in Washington are being pressurized to accept, since they are negotiating from a position of extreme weakness. The Palestinians have nothing to offer which they can use to bargain for better terms.

16 February 1993

It was a cold and sunny day with snow-covered mountains dazzlingly white in the sun. The men had been staging a mock funeral, holding aloft the coffin of the United Nations. They see the UN as having failed them completely with 'watery' resolution and double standards. The demonstration had been shown on Lebanese and Israeli TV, prompting some who had only caught a glimpse to believe that one of the exiles had died. They laughingly reassured us that they are all in reasonably good health.

We discussed the station's needs with Dr Zyad. They really would prefer to have money so that they can buy what they need from the villages nearby. With Ramadan drawing near they particularly want to buy some of the sheep and cows which are grazing around them. The villagers obviously feel it is safe to come to the station now, even in daylight.

There has been a three-day international conference in Beirut to discuss the question of the exiles and one of the Jordanian delegates came to visit. Of course he emphasised the obvious point that since there is no oil in Marj al Zahour nor in Lebanon the West is not really concerned about the plight of the exiles.

2 March 1993

Seventy-five of the exiles are from Hebron and today it was their turn to prepare the Ramadan meal for everybody. When we arrived, lamb, rice and *leban* (yoghurt), purchased with money gifted to them, were cooking in the enormous pots donated by the International Red Cross when the men were first exiled. There is someone skilled in everything that the men need at Marj al Zahour — slaughterers, cooks, plumbers, barbers, doctors, nurses, teachers, professors and sheikhs.

The range of subjects being offered by the University of Ibn Taimih has been expanded to include biology, first aid and even Hebrew. They therefore need books — each member of the press corps brings in a book and they are building up a library.

6 March 1993

Today was cold and dull but spring has begun in Marj al Zahour with the appearance of the first red anemones — they always remind me of spring in Nazareth. One of the exiles had set up his easel and was painting the panorama of snow-capped mountains and the fresh green of the fields.

Some of the men had taken advantage of the three-hour library opening and were sitting reading in the library tent, while the librarian was busy cataloguing the 200 or so books on all kinds of subjects, including a Bible, which had been donated. One of the men is a poet and composes songs, expressing their longing for home, which they sing responsively.

16 April 1993

This was the end of the fourth month of exile so a demonstration was staged to mark the date. We arrived early so we were able to march with the men to the Zamriyeh crossing, controlled by the Israeli and the South Lebanese armies. There were a number of other people from the press walking with us. After the men had prayed and listened to a sermon, we set off at a slow pace along the road. It was a scorching hot day, but the men were well prepared with drinking water, three first aid teams, a stretcher bearer and even onions for the expected tear gas.

As we came in sight of the gate at the crossing we could see soldiers, tanks and water cannon on the hillside. Shots were fired into the surrounding hills, and, as we advanced, bullets ricocheted off the rocks. We just sat down in the road when there was shooting. I overheard a Lebanese cub reporter say, 'I wonder what my mother would be thinking if she knew I was here.' The men had brought food so, presently, in one of the lulls they shared their food with the press corps, a real feeding of the 5,000 in the wilderness. We reached a point slightly nearer to the crossing than on their first march. Only one man was injured, receiving a superficial wound on the chest from a splinter of rock. The aim of the march was to try and press the Arab leaders, then meeting in Syria, not to agree to join the peace negotiations without extracting concessions from Israel about exile and the closure of the Occupied Territories.

30 April 1993

Today we found the men still encamped on the road in sight of the military forces at the Zamriyeh crossing. They have decided to stay on the road 'until further notice'. There has been no further firing, but powerful searchlights are directed nightly on them and obscene remarks about Dr Ghantisi are shouted through a loud hailer. The men are, as usual, well organised. The food is cooked in the main camp and brought out to the men, as are their medicines, but otherwise they sit on the road all the time. There is very little shade, only a few scattered olive trees in the fields at the side of the road. We joined them at breakfast time and were given cups of tea. Formal classes in the university are suspended but informal teaching, of course, goes on, as does regular Koranic teaching. The Arab Council for Higher Education has agreed to accept all the examination results from the Ibn Taimih University, which is great news for the men.

20 May 1993

We began our visit today in the clinic tent and heard a report on the visit of three doctors from Jordan, one a professor of orthopaedics. He had examined eighty-four men and found fifteen in need of urgent treatment for torn knee menisci, a result of having to walk on the rough terrain.

One of the most serious cases is that of a man diagnosed as having schizophrenia. The doctors have requested that the International Red Cross should negotiate for his repatriation as soon as possible. Fortunately most of the time he is quiet and well controlled. One of the doctors is 'knocking up' a shed, from wood he found lying around, in which to keep all their medical equipment — needless to say it does not have to be a very big shed.

The men have formed a football team and are playing matches with the nearby Lebanese villages, on a pitch situated just as far into Lebanon as they are permitted to go. A team of exiled doctors played a team of exiled engineers at volleyball — the engineers won three to one, but the doctors were quick to point out that they are older! Before we left we were treated to a cold drink from the little shop, a co-operative they have set up, selling fresh fruit, mosquito coils and cold drinks among other things, bought in from the nearby Lebanese villages. I chatted to the 'manager' who is the accountant at the National Hotel in Jerusalem. He graduated from the University of Wales and is an expert on financial management.

There is still snow on Mount Hermon which keeps the temperature bearable but the mosquitos are very troublesome at night. The museum is filling up with specimens which they have pickled (including twenty different varieties of snakes) — they asked us to bring in some formalin and we could not imagine why!

The men were cheered by a video which had been sent in about the 'Peace Now' Movement in Israel, depicting how Muslims, Christians and Jews are campaigning on their behalf.

12 June 1993

This was my first visit for five weeks so it was good to see my friends again. They were in good heart and the choir were busy practising some new songs. They have spread their tents up the hill over a wide area in order to catch more air. They have to be constantly vigilant for scorpions and snakes.

Outside the big clinic tent there is now a large notice board set up giving information about all lectures and courses available. This week there is to be a lecture on, 'How to keep healthy in the heat of summer'. There are now classes in four languages, English, Hebrew, German and Spanish.

3 July 1993

Today was very hot and sticky. The men asked wistfully if August would be as hot as July — it will be. Our medical supplies and sunglasses were very welcome as was a 1993 edition of a medical textbook. The doctors are hungry for something to read. They had done two minor operations that morning, one patient being a Lebanese villager.

Their water is inadequate, so it is difficult for them to wash the dishes or the vegetables properly, and conservation of fuel prohibits the boiling of water, so many of them are suffering from diarrhoea. However they treated us to lunch of lentil soup, vegetable stew and salad, and we suffered no ill effects.

25 July 1993

All the men were having a picnic in the hills when we arrived today, so we joined them and sat under an olive tree sharing their lunch of mutton and rice. We then drove back to the station, at least Dr Zayd drove Dr Yoga's car, a real treat for him after months of exile, then we all enjoyed a cold drink in the shop.

We collected some laboratory specimens to take back to Rashidia Hospital, and a litre of fresh blood from Ramadan, the singing 'bard', who has too many red blood cells, causing him severe headaches. The soldiers at the checkpoint on our way were distinctly nonplussed but we said that it was better that we give it to a hospital, rather than throwing it away and, as things turned out, it was useful with the outbreak of war the next day. We heard the planes and some firing but did not know how extensive and severe Israel's attacks had been until we got back to Beirut in the evening.

7 August 1993

We visited today to see how the men had fared during the war. They had, of course, heard the bombardment, but it had not come near them and they had still been able to get food supplies.

They told us about the possibility of a 'piecemeal' return home, first on 17 September the eighty-two who are in need of medical treatment and then 100 every month until the last group on 17 December. They have agreed that, as they have made their point by withstanding such a long exile, they would not now insist on going back together. How they will actually get back is still not clear as both Lebanon and Israel are refusing to let them cross the borders. Whether they will return to their homes or to prison is another uncertainty, but they are counting the days anyway as it will be a step nearer home.

22 August 1993

The highlight today was seeing two fifty-four-year-old headmasters playing ping-pong on their newly-acquired table which they have set up in the mosque tent. Other men were sitting around reading. Abu Mousa, the dean of the university, was in the 'office' taking registrations for the next semester. Nobody ever seems to be idle in Marj al Zahour!

9 September 1993

This was the day for 180 of the exiles to cross the border, on the first leg of their return home, knowing that they will face interrogation by the Israeli authorities, but, nevertheless rejoicing. We were able to walk with them to the border gate and see them being 'ticked off' on the Israeli side. It was an emotional scene, as those having to stay behind embraced their fellows with whom they had spent nine months of exile.

17 September 1993

Because they are now a smaller number they have, symbolically, folded up nine of the tents. They were able to give us good news of those who had gone back. They had heard by means of the mobile phone link they have set up. The returning men had been treated much more humanely on their journey back — they were handcuffed, but not with steel bands, and they were given food and water and their guards joked with them, saying that they were not police but waiters! After ninety-five hours of interrogation, ninety were allowed to go home, but those who had been taken from prison were returned to prison.

Dr Omar has compiled some demographic statistics — 108 babies were born during the exile, fifty-six females and sixty-two males with one stillbirth and one death. Dr Omar said very seriously, 'There will be no more babies now.'

15 October 1993

Today we heard that Dr Azeez, one of the exiles and a geologist, has discovered an ancient castle which he dates from Roman times, around 200 BC. He also found Byzantine and early Islamic coins. They have notified the Lebanese authorities but, so far, no-one has come to investigate. Maybe they are waiting until all the exiles have gone home.

7 November 1993

Today we heard that the Lebanese government archaeologists had questioned Dr Azeez about his findings. He was firmly told that as he is only a 'tourist', he is not allowed to go wandering around the hills, excavating. He was forced to sign a paper that he would not go near the site again nor take any visitor to see it. We were very disappointed as we had hoped to go.

27 November 1993

Today the fruit trees were a gorgeous display of reds and browns.

The brother of one of the HAMAS activists killed recently in Israel is one of the exiles, so there was sorrow among the men although the dead man is considered a martyr. When the Israelis cannot catch the man they want they imprison the wanted man's brother instead, and a number of the men in exile in Marj al Zahour are there because it was their brothers the authorities really wanted. The majority of the exiles have still not been formally charged with any crime.

3 December 1993

Hopefully our last visit, although there is still no official word. The men had prepared a delicious lunch for us, fried chicken, stuffed vine leaves and salad. They had remembered that I do not like mutton so had prepared the chicken specially!

14/15 December 1993

This was D-Day for the exiles at last! On the evening of 14 December 1993 we drove through fog and snow to Marj al Zahour, having heard on Israel radio that the men were to return the next day. The camp was already a hive of activity with crowds of journalists milling around. It was a beautiful, clear moonlit night but very cold and exceedingly muddy underfoot. Dr Omar gave us the use of his tent for the night and Mary and I were later joined by two French journalists. We sat by the gas fire and watched a TV programme from Rome featuring many Christian paintings, including the Crucifixion and accompanied by classical religious music. We thought what strange entertainment to be enjoying in the tent of an ardent Islamic exile! Fortunately he was not there as all the men were busy packing up and saying their goodbyes. I slept well but at 5 am we were awakened by the Call to Prayer and by the Lebanese villagers coming to collect the blankets! At 7 am we joined the men as they set off for the border crossing. The camp was then quickly dismantled by the Lebanese villagers who had befriended them during their long exile — the first Palestinian camp to be taken down! Each man carried one bag. Around 8 am the Israeli security men arrived at the border gate with a few soldiers, in civilian clothes but armed. They deployed themselves around the gate, having made a futile search of an empty barn. Dr Ghantisi was called and he crossed over and was received quite cordially and helped in calling out the names. The whole crossing was completed in about an hour. Eighteen chose to stay and 'disappear' in Lebanon, with the connivance of the Lebanese authorities, rather than face life imprisonment in Israel.

So ended quite a saga — we were sad to say goodbye to our friends but, of course, glad that they were one step nearer home. Who knows if and when we will see them again. We were glad that we had been able to stand alongside them during their ordeal and grateful to MAP, ODA (who provided the funds for our 'mercy mission') and the newspaper which provided us with our legitimacy to be members of the press corps.

I was in Scotland at Christmas so was able to telephone to Dr Omar in Gaza and learn that all but seventeen of the exiles had reached their homes safely.

I visited Gaza in November 1994 and met with Dr Omar. He did not want to talk about his time of exile which he said was the longest and the hardest experience of his life. He was keen for me to meet his family, to see his medical work and to take me around Gaza, no longer harassed by Israeli soldiers. He told me that he had decided to stick to his medical work and not get involved in politics. He is doing a wonderful medical job, running a number of clinics in Gaza for the benefit of the really poor people. These are well-equipped clinics, with a team of like-minded doctors.

1 (Copyright ©1973, 1978, 1984 by the International Bible Society. Used by permission of Hodder & Stoughton Ltd. All rights reserved.)

2 *Btselem-Deportation of Palestines* (Jerusalem-Israeli Information Centre for Human Rights in the Occupied Territories, 1993, p. 7)

18

RELIGION

'Religion that God our Father accepts as pure and faithful is this;
to look after orphans and widows in their distress.'

James 1.27 (New International Version of the Holy Bible)[1]

The three Abrahamic faiths trace their beginnings to Jerusalem — but which Jerusalem? A Jerusalem 'to be a delight and its
people a joy'[2] as envisaged by the Prophet Isaiah or Jerusalem, a
divided city?

Jerusalem for Christians, is where God manifested Himself cru-
cially and quite literally on Golgotha, to redeem the world. Noisy,
it may be, crowded, quarrelled over and, to some eyes, even a bit
tawdry, yet I cannot be in Jerusalem without my feet taking me to
the Church of the Holy Sepulchre to pray, the church called by
Orthodox Christians, much more realistically, the Church of the
Resurrection — for we worship a living Saviour.

Jerusalem for the Jewish people, is the site of the Temple, first
Solomon's, then Herod's and the great Herodian stones of the
Second Temple are part of the Western Wall. Jerusalem, insist the
Israelis, is the eternal capital of Israel.

Jerusalem for Muslims, was the first *qibla* to which the Muslims turned in prayer. When Mecca was still in the hands of the
pagans and the *Ka'ba* full of idols, the Prophet knew that Jerusalem was a holy city to the Christians and to the Jews, and so he
had no option but to instruct his followers to turn to Jerusalem
until Mecca had been liberated. Jerusalem thus came to be seen as
their third most sacred place.

Jerusalem, the holy city in the Holy Land, where I lived and
worked for forty years has become a very meaningful symbol to
me of the three monotheistic faiths.

When I think of Islam I think first of a Muslim friend saying
to me, 'I wish you were a Muslim, then you too could go to paradise' — loving me enough to sorrow at my fate as a Christian.
Then I think of a Muslim teacher, a patient of mine in Nazareth. I

prescribed for her a regime of strict bed rest, but she said, 'How can I be off school, who will look after the children in my class?' Only then do I think of *Jehad* (in Arabic 'to struggle'), a word which strikes terror into the hearts of so many in the West, those who know little about Islam and do not take the trouble to find out nor to meet any Muslims. In the Koran it says, 'Fight in the way of Allah against those who fight against you, but begin not hostilities lo, Allah loveth not aggressors.'[3]

It is helpful to know that, 'The principle of *Jehad* developed because it dealt directly with the exercise of armed coercive power which is at the heart of any state and, in particular, the Islamic state as understood by traditional Islamic consciousness.'[4] Islam is not only a religion, it is a whole way of life and a political system, so it acts like any state. Until we in the erstwhile Christian states and in Israel — the only Jewish state — forgo armed aggression and the possession of nuclear weapons, we are in no position to lambast Islamic states.

Yaseen is a devout Muslim, a Sunni, but perhaps verging towards Shi'ism, and we were talking one day about the West's fear of Islam and why it is so afraid. He suggested it is because the West does not know what real Islam is. He said that real Islam wants peace and he claimed that Indonesia became Islamic only a century ago and that this arose from 'preaching', not by the sword. Like most Palestinians in Lebanon he would love the chance to emigrate to the West, for the future of his children, but also so that he could show the West what he sees as 'real Islam'— equality between Muslims and non-Muslims so that there would be no reason to fear Islam.

There is, it cannot be denied, armed struggle. Hizbullah is fighting Israel and its surrogate army in south Lebanon, a struggle they see as quite legitimate as Israel is the aggressor having invaded and occupied Lebanon. So Hizbullah launches punitive raids and Israel retaliates. The Lebanese Shi'ites support, or tolerate, Hizbullah in their midst as they too want to rid Lebanon of the occupiers. Hizbullah is not only a military organisation — there are eight Hizbullah deputies in the Lebanese parliament and they have very active social programmes including one of the best hospitals in Beirut.

Islam, ever since the Crusades, believes that Christianity, the West and the Western values they perceive as originating from

Christianity, is a militant and aggressive religion, bent on defeating and humiliating Islam. They think that it is a religion which only cares 'for its own' and they cite the tragedy of Bosnia. They believe that the West does not want a Muslim state in the middle of Europe, so that is why nothing is done to help the Bosnian Muslims. Once again fear and ignorance blind and paralyse people — Islam fearing Western Christianity and the West fearing militant Islam.

It is impossible to live and work among Muslims without being very aware of the five pillars of Islam, by which their lives are regulated, and to see their almost universal observance — people really do stop what they are doing to pray five times a day, they do fast at Ramadan, they do give alms if they are able, they do proclaim their faith once in their lifetime and they do all long to be able to make the *Hajj* (the pilgrimage to Mecca during the last month of the Muslim year). Just before I left Qasmiyeh in 1994, my neighbour, Im Fahmi, a widow and her unmarried daughter, Miriam, wanted to go to Mecca. It is forbidden for any unmarried woman to go unless with her brother. All Miriam's brothers are living in Germany so she was temporarily married 'on paper' to the uncle who was going to escort them. On the day of their departure they had to dress in the obligatory white garments and we all gathered to speed them on their way.

The *Hajj* is a real endurance test — millions of pilgrims, heat, dust and walking and walking. The travel and accommodation are carefully arranged and the pilgrims are housed together with fellow pilgrims from their country of origin, for, of course, they come from all over the world. Very wisely every pilgrim is issued with a wrist band on which the name and the hotel where they are staying is written, a wise precaution as Miriam unfortunately became separated from her mother but was later reunited. It was a miracle to me that Im Fahmi, who is in her sixties, survived and completed the whole of the *Hajj*. Death during this pilgrimage is considered to be a blessing as it means instant entrance to paradise — hundreds, some say thousands of pilgrims from Nigeria were crushed to death when a balcony on which some were standing gave way and fell on those standing below. One of Im Fahmi's sons travelled specially from Germany to Qasmiyeh to prepare the welcome home for his mother and sister. He paved the entrance to their house, previously a muddy path, and erected an arch painted with congratulatory slogans decorated with flowers. They arrived home safely albeit exhausted, but renewed. The *Hajj* carries a most definite meaning — it is not a holiday, nor a picnic, it is not just a ritual and not only an obligation, it should be a profound spiritual experience. Im Fahmi and Miriam returned radiant, saying they had been through a process of purification and felt reborn and should never again say anything bad about other people.

I see Judaism like an hour glass — God is the Creator of all things in heaven and earth, then He chose the Jews to be the line through which He would send the Saviour, the Messiah, to save His people from their sins, so the glass narrowed. In the fullness of time, with the coming of Christ and His message of salvation for all peoples the glass opens up again widely, to encompass everybody. It seems to me significant that the concept of a 'promised land' does not figure in the New Testament, 'the earth is the Lord's'. The Jews however, have 'stayed with the veils over their faces'. As St Paul writes, '...To this day the same veil remains when the old covenant is read. It has not been removed, because only in Christ is it taken away ... but whenever anyone turns to the Lord, the veil is taken away.'[5]

Zionism and Israel grew out of European anti-semitism, most immediately from the trumped up imprisonment of Alfred Dreyfus in France which convinced Herzl that there could be no future for the Jews in Europe — they must have a country of their own. European anti-semitism, culminating in the Holocaust, has given the West such a burden of guilt — because it did nothing to stop it and then closed its doors to the survivors — that it applies to Israel 'the law of exception'. This gives Israel special rights not accorded to others. Thus the US, and usually the UK, veto all UN resolutions that censure Israel and if they do get passed Israel is allowed to ignore them with impunity.

The North American theologian, Rosemary Ruether, explains the confusion that has arisen between classical Judaism and the modern nation-state which Israel has become. She writes, 'When Zionism first arose the vast majority of the leaders of all forms of Judaism rejected it as contrary to their understanding of Judaism. For Orthodox Jews, Zionism was an unholy project carried out by non-observant Jews and thus fundamentally contradictory to their religious belief in a Messianic restoration of political sover-

eignty over the ancient homeland. For the Orthodox, this restoration could only take place as an expression of a redemptive process. This meant the redemption of the Jews and a complementary
redemption of all nations. It meant a restoration that would heal
the enmity between the nations and bring world peace.'[6]

On the contrary, the birth of Israel heralded years and decades
of war and suffering in the whole of the Middle East. By their
ruthlessness they have betrayed their Judaism — I always think
of a Jewish friend who brought his elderly mother from South
Africa to live near him in Israel. He said to me once after the
outbreak of the Intifada, 'Mom is driving me crazy — she keeps
asking me, are these people Jews, and when I say yes, of course
they are Jews, she says no, they cannot be, Jews do not do things
like that.' She was referring to the pictures on television of the
way the Israeli army were treating the stone-throwing youngsters.

Even today, after all that has happened, most Palestinians whom
I know would be prepared to live with Jews as their neighbours
although they will never be able to understand why their country
had to be given to the Jews to expiate the guilt of the West. In
contrast, a friend in Gaza told me that Jewish friends of hers had
told her that they would be afraid of living as neighbours with
Palestinians after the way the Israeli army and the settlers have
treated the Palestinians — they fear revenge.

The Holy Land has never been a land of only one people, but
a land of many peoples. Abu Samr in Qasmiyeh agrees, 'the earth
is the Lord's and the fullness thereof,' but, he says, 'The problem
is that the Israelis want to make a land exclusively for Jews —
how can they call that a democracy? We Palestinians want to share
it with them and live alongside them as neighbours — for us that
would not be a problem!'

1   *New International Version of the Holy Bible* (Copyright © 1973, 1978, 1984 by Internat-
    tional Bible Society. Used by permission Hodder & Stoughton Ltd. All rights reserved.)
2   *Isaiah 65.18, New International Version of the Holy Bible*
3   *Holy Koran, Sura 2* (trs. of Abdulla Yusuf Ali, Beirut, Dar al Arabia, 1934)
4   *Abdulla Schleifer* (Islamic Quarterly Vol. I No. 27, Islamic Cultural Centre, London, 1983,
    p.179)
5   *2 Corinthians 3.14 and 15, New International Version of the Holy Bible*
6   Rosemary Ruether, *Faith And The Intifada* (Orbis Books, New York, 1992, p.152)

19

EPILOGUE

'To dance at the margins
and to see
the face of Christ
where hurt is real and
pain a way of life.
To be touched
in the eye of the storm,
aware that tomorrow
may not bring peace.'

Peter Millar[1]

The best stories always have a happy ending and the story of the Palestinians is an ongoing story with no end in sight. Certainly there have been the Oslo Accords, the idea behind them being that Palestine should be partitioned, as it should have been under the terms of UN Resolution 242 of 1967, perhaps with minor adjustments, but with equal rights of independence and self-government for both Israel and Palestine (within an agreed time scale). This might have been possible but for the settlements planted, by successive Israeli governments, all over the Occupied Territories; and it might still have been possible if the present Israeli government had possessed the will and the strength to discipline the settlers. The real responsibility for the failure rests on the world community and principally on the US. It is the only government which can make Israel decide whether it wants peace or territory. Even if, and when, there is some movement on the future of the Occupied Territories, the 250,000 Palestinians living in Lebanon are still stateless.

This, however, is the story of people I love and admire for their courage, tenacity and resilience through years of suffering, so I cannot close on a note of despair — I owe it to them to continue to hope. Most of the time they are not in despair, they are getting on with the job of living.

Some Palestinians still believe in the armed struggle, but many say that the revolution has failed, their leaders have betrayed them but that they must continue the struggle, albeit unarmed. How is this to be done?

My friend Mary Khass, an erstwhile Communist but then a Quaker died very suddenly at her home in Gaza in May 1995. Her death is a real tragedy for the Palestinian cause because she believed in the way of active nonviolence. She said to me, 'Since 1948 the Palestinians have never been winners. Politically nonviolence is the only way forward.' She lived and worked in Gaza and set up a Ghandi Centre to teach the Ghandian principles of active nonviolence. There, amidst all the squalor and horror and suffering of Gaza she lit a beacon of light which, hopefully, she has left bravely burning.

Dr Hatim Kinaaneh, Director of the Galilee Society, is working for equal rights for the Palestinians who are citizens of Israel and live within the Green Line. Israel has a new policy which they call 'Judaizing the Galilee'. One of the first things they have done is to move a big glass factory from Haifa to a site near Nazareth. Glass factories are notorious for producing pollution. The GSHRS took the factory owner to court. He had no building permit but was issued one within twenty-four hours although it usually takes months to get a permit! They could not prevent the move but they did win an out-of-court order for strict controls over polluting emissions. The local councils of the nearby villages were warned that they would lose their government grants if they joined the campaign, so the Galilee Society, as an independent NGO 'went it alone'.

Many Beduin living in Galilee and in the Negev are still struggling for their rights as Israeli citizens. They live in what the government call 'illegal settlements', where they have lived for generations, and are continually being threatened with removal. The Galilee Society has campaigned vigorously for those in Galilee with some success and are now providing a mobile health clinic for those living in the Negev. So the struggle for equality goes on.

Mary Khass also recognised the crying need for real democracy in the new 'Gaza/Jericho First', which it was agreed at Oslo would be the first autonomous Palestinian area, so, as well as the Ghandi Centre, she set up a programme to teach the meaning of democracy to young Gazans alongside young Israelis. She ran seminars for the two peoples to meet and get to know each other and thus destroy the stereotypes which years of harsh occupation had produced. I pray that the seeds Mary has sown will take root and bear fruit.

Cedar Daibes of Ramallah is a member of Sabeel, the Palestinian Liberation Theology Centre in Jerusalem (*Sabeel* is Arabic for 'a way' and also 'a spring'). The Centre attempts to help Palestinian Christians to practice theology in their daily lives, and to find theologically-based answers to their questions of how one can live under occupation and maintain one's faith? How can one not lose hope? What is God saying to us today? They are also working with young people encouraging inter-faith tolerance and coexistence. They hope to be able to produce a unified school curriculum that can be used by Muslims, Jews and Christians in the future.

Dr Salah is director of medical services for the PRCS in south Lebanon and a man of the greatest integrity. He played a vital role during the sieges of Rashidia in 1982 and 1987 and in the 'Camp Wars' when he was the only doctor. He says, 'God must have been with us, we had no sterility and no gloves yet patients survived. The nurses were marvellous, we all pulled together, but it was hard to go on living as friends and family members were killed around us all the time.' Now he says, 'The revolution has failed, so education is the best and the only way forward for us. The Israelis have succeeded, not because of their number, but because they are highly educated and very clever and so have been able to influence the US.'

It is good to see young Palestinians in Lebanon looking for education — perhaps they hope it will open doors for emigration, but it is also a genuine love of learning.

Jamileh Khawalid is the co-ordinator of Educational Projects for Beit Atfal Samood (an NGO in Lebanon, largely run by women), which has programmes for children and young people between four and nineteen years old. They have recently started the 'child-to-child' programme, asking the mothers 'What do you want to know' and the children 'What do you want to learn?', and always teaching them what it means to be a Palestinian. Jamileh imbued her younger sister, Najah, with the thirst for education too; Jamileh brought her up, as their mother died in childbirth and their father was killed in the fighting. They live in Shatila camp in Beirut and

Najah has a degree in psychology from the Arab University in Beirut and then she was awarded the Glasgow University students' bursary to study Nursing Management. She is now teaching in the PRCS Nursing School in Sidon.

Rehab Daher, who used to work with me, is the best student in her class in the Hariri Nursing School in Sidon. It was Rehab who said to me one day, 'You know Doctora, I cannot hate anyone'. Her father was killed in the fighting when she was very small. Her smiling face always makes me think of the words of Jesus in St Matthew's Gospel. 'The eye is the lamp of the body. If your eyes are good, your whole body will be full of light.'[2]

Dr Khalil Toucan of Jenin, in the Occupied Territories, has managed to send two of his children to university, one to Baghdad and one to Jordan. These are youngsters who grew up in the Intifada. Raid, his son, spent time in prison when he was fifteen, so it is difficult for them to settle down to study now. Their father encourages them: 'If you are rich you never reach (meaning you are never satisfied), but if you are poor you struggle.'

There is, however, the great and ever present danger that the best education in the world is ineffective in getting things changed if the well educated do not have political power. I fear that this is happening in Nazareth, where there is an educated Palestinian population which has very little say in the running of the country and for whom there are job restrictions because of the exclusiveness of the state of Israel. So people then turn to making money, with the result that Nazareth is one of the most materialistic places I know, as bad as any place in the West and becoming equally inward looking and selfish.

The love found within the close-knit Palestinian family is still very strong. Some might say that the children are spoilt, but the parents are completely selfless — when it comes to the crunch they willingly let them go. They realise that there is no future for young Palestinians in Lebanon so, if the opportunity arises, they let them emigrate, even actively encourage them. They know that in their declining years they will be alone and their lives may only be lightened by telephone calls (many of the older generation are illiterate) and visits from their loved ones in the summer.

Dr Salah suddenly asked me one day, 'Do you believe in God?' I replied, 'Yes, I could never have done what I have been able to do if I had not had a firm faith in God, and it is my faith that keeps me going even though things do look bleak.' He said that he, too, had only been able to survive throughout the years of the civil war in Lebanon and to participate in the struggles of his people because he believed in God. He is a Muslim, I am a Christian, we have our different beliefs and ways of worshipping God, but we both believe in a God of Justice and Mercy.

'In You, O God of life I place my hope
My great hope, my living hope, this day and evermore.'

An ancient Celtic morning prayer. [3]

1   *Daily Thoughts from a Columban House* (Newtonmore, 1994, day 21)
2   *Matthew 6.22, New International Version of the Holy Bible* (Copyright © 1973, 1978, 1984 by International Bible Society. Used by permission Hodder & Stoughton Ltd. All rights reserved.)
3   *Carmina Gadelica* (Floris Books, Edinburgh, 1992)

MEDICAL AID
FOR PALESTINIANS

Medical Aid for Palestinians is an independent British-registered charity established in 1984 after the Sabra and Shatila massacres 'for the relief of poverty and sickness and the advancement of education amongst refugees ... displaced from the former British Mandate of Palestine.'

MAP's priority is the provision of training programmes for Palestinian health personnel working in hospitals, clinics and the community. MAP is working to support the development of a comprehensive health infrastructure for the Palestinian population but at the same time maintains the ability to respond to emergencies.

MAP works with over thirty local NGOs in Lebanon, the West Bank and Gaza, and co-operates with other international organisations including Save the Children Fund, Norwegian Aid Committee, UNICEF and UNRWA, etc.

Over 350 specialised health and medical volunteers have been sent by MAP to Lebanon, the Occupied Territories and Egypt in the last ten years.

There is still much work to be done.

Please complete and return to :

MAP, 33A Islington Park Street, London N1 1QB

I would like further information about MAP's work, please send me:

..... Your latest newsletter

..... MAP's fundraising sheet

..... A Deed of Covenant form

..... Add my name and address to your mailing list. I would like
    to receive regular news about MAP's work and fundraising events.

THE IONA COMMUNITY

The Iona Community was founded in 1938 by the late Lord MacLeod of Fuinary (the Rev. George MacLeod DD). It was initially a movement for renewal in the Church of Scotland. The rebuilding of the ruined cloistral buildings of Iona Abbey (completed, through a combination of professional and voluntary work over nearly thirty years, in 1967) provided a powerful focus for the specific concerns of the Community: the integration of work and worship, politics and prayer, and the development of new forms of worship, of the common life, of youth work, of the ministry of healing, and of experiments in mission.

The Community today is a movement of some 200 members, 1200 associates and 2000 friends. It describes itself as 'an ecumenical community, within the Church of Scotland, of men and women seeking new ways of living the Gospel in today's world.' Its members are committed to a rule of daily prayer and Bible study, sharing and accounting for the use of their money and their time, meeting together, and action for peace and justice in the world.

The Community maintains three centres of work, worship, and the common life on Iona and Mull, and administrative offices in Glasgow.

Please complete and return to:
The Iona Community, Pearce Institute, 840 Govan Road, Glasgow
G51 3UU; Tel: 0141 440 4561; Fax: 0141 445 4295.

I would like further information about the Iona Community's work. Please send me:
....   Membership details
....   A Deed of Covenant form
....   Information about volunteering on Iona
....   A catalogue of publications

OTHER TITLES FROM WILD GOOSE PUBLICATIONS

SONGBOOKS with full music (titles marked * have companion cassettes)
COME ALL YOU PEOPLE, Shorter Songs for Worship* John Bell
PSALMS OF PATIENCE, PROTEST AND PRAISE* John Bell
HEAVEN SHALL NOT WAIT (Wild Goose Songs Vol.1)* John Bell & Graham Maule
ENEMY OF APATHY (Wild Goose Songs Vol.2) John Bell and Graham Maule
LOVE FROM BELOW (Wild Goose Songs Vol.3)* John Bell and Graham Maule
INNKEEPERS & LIGHT SLEEPERS* (for Christmas) JohnBell
MANY & GREAT (Songs of the World Church Vol.1)* John Bell (ed./arr.)
SENT BY THE LORD (Songs of the World Church Vol.2)* John Bell (ed./arr.)
FREEDOM IS COMING* Anders Nyberg (ed.)
PRAISING A MYSTERY, Brian Wren
BRING MANY NAMES, Brian Wren

CASSETTES & CDs (titles marked † have companion songbooks)
Tape, COME ALL YOU PEOPLE, † Wild Goose Worship Group
CD, PSALMS OF PATIENCE, PROTEST AND PRAISE, WGWG
Tape, PSALMS OF PATIENCE, PROTEST AND PRAISE, WGWG
Tape, HEAVEN SHALL NOT WAIT† WGWG
Tape, LOVE FROM BELOW† WGWG
Tape, INNKEEPERS & LIGHT SLEEPERS† (for Christmas) WGWG
Tape, MANY & GREAT† WGWG
Tape, SENT BY THE LORD† WGWG
Tape, FREEDOM IS COMING† Fjedur
Tape, TOUCHING PLACE, A, WGWG
Tape, CLOTH FOR THE CRADLE, WGWG

DRAMA BOOKS
EH JESUS...YES PETER No. 1, John Bell and Graham Maule
EH JESUS...YES PETER No. 2, John Bell and Graham Maule
EH JESUS...YES PETER No. 3, John Bell and Graham Maule
WILD GOOSE PRINTS No. 1, John Bell and Graham Maule
WILD GOOSE PRINTS No. 2, John Bell and Graham Maule
WILD GOOSE PRINTS No. 3, John Bell and Graham Maule
WILD GOOSE PRINTS No. 4 (On the way to the cross), John Bell & Graham Maule
WILD GOOSE PRINTS No. 5, John Bell and Graham Maule
WILD GOOSE PRINTS No. 6 (Christmas scripts) John Bell and Graham Maule

PRAYER/WORSHIP BOOKS
PRAYERS AND IDEAS FOR HEALING SERVICES, Ian Cowie
HE WAS IN THE WORLD, Meditations for Public Worship, John Bell
EACH DAY AND EACH NIGHT, Prayers from Iona ..., Philip Newell
IONA COMMUNITY WORSHIP BOOK, THE
WEE WORSHIP BOOK, A, Wild Goose Worship Group
WHOLE EARTH SHALL CRY GLORY, THE, George MacLeod

OTHER BOOKS
FALLEN TO MEDIOCRITY: CALLED TO EXCELLENCE, Erik Cramb
RE-INVENTING THEOLOGY AS THE PEOPLE'S WORK, Ian Fraser
ROGER, An extraordinary Peace Campaigner, Helen Steven
WAY TO GOD, A – A biography of George More, Mary More